Pathfinders

D. Bruce Howell, PhD

Pathfinders

19th Century Pioneers of Cherokee Territory

D. Bruce Howell, PhD

Pathfinders

Copyright @2016 by D. Bruce Howell, PhD

All rights reserved.

ISDN: 978-1539965961

First Edition: December, 2016

Table of Contents

Introduction

The men that were selected as Pathfinders in this publication represent just a cross section of pioneers who initially shaped Cherokee Territory. They originated from all walks of life and, over time, arrived with varied agendas. Some came for business purposes, some were intent upon developing the region as a nation, others strove to educate and protect its citizens and a few simply contributed to its infrastructure before moving on to another project. Their combined contributions resulted in the initiation of a fledgling country that, under a different set of circumstances, might have survived today as the entity that was envisioned.

The biographies of these Pathfinders are a composite of thousands who saw Cherokee Territory as a land of opportunity. Looking back on their resoluteness and accomplishments, their deeds in the face of adversity are nearly incomprehensible in comparison to the luxuries of living we are afforded today. Some arrived with a wagon load of their dearest possessions, others with just the clothes on their back, but as generations pass it has become evident that most survived and prospered.

Family names such as Adair, Rogers, and Martin are among many that are reminders of current generations with ties to the past. Even more apparent are the values and characteristics of the old settlers that have been passed on both through actions and appearances. The small churches that dot the countryside bear evidence of the fruits of the labors of "God's Emissaries" mentioned in Chapter Five. The values of the "Nation Builders" in Chapter Six are reflected by the work ethic of current citizens and the distinct features of many of those chosen to be included, remind us of the Cherokee heritage that still permeates the region.

Although considerable differences in the traditional or integrated lifestyles of its citizens divided them at the time, the Cherokee Nation and its founders made significant strides from 1839 until the Civil War. A constitution was ratified and the Nation was divided into eight districts with representatives forming the National Council and National Committee. A capitol and Supreme Court building were constructed in Tahlequah. A national treasury was founded and judicial and law enforcement systems were in place in each of the districts. The *Cherokee Advocate* printed in both Cherokee and English was founded in 1844 and a system of education was developed that by 1859 included 30 schools attended by 1,500 students.

But earlier circumstances were also pervasive that laid the foundation for failure. A charter designating land dedicated to "Indian Territory" was initiated by a federal government that lacked both the will and the resources to develop it. Then while the concept was just beginning to evolve into a stable government, the Cherokee Nation was torn apart by not just one but two insurmountable issues, the Civil War and a festering disagreement over the circumstances leading to removal from the East that had no solution. The Civil War divided the Nation on the pragmatic issue of slavery, an issue that eventually was resolved by the victorious Union. But the internal disagreement stemming from the Treaty of New Echota divided the Nation philosophically and is still fodder for debate.

Although these issues created turmoil within the Cherokee citizenry other internal obstacles also confronted them. There were porous borders that enabled anyone to enter, overlapping federal statutes that diluted the sovereignty of the Nation and prevented equal law enforcement among residents. These circumstances were abetted by an underfinanced government that could not support its schools, government agencies or infrastructure.

Then there were the external post war factors. Indian Territory had aligned itself with the Confederacy and was punished as a result. Unlike the southern Confederacy, no reconstruction assistance was provided nor did post war negotiations resolve issues. Instead, almost immediately the United States Congress began deliberating the efficacy of dividing the region into one or two states. Soon, over protests of the Cherokee government, two railroads were approved to reach across the Nation. Within 25 years after the Civil War land runs were permitted in Indian Territory and shortly thereafter a process of division was initiated through the Dawes Commission contrary to the Indian tradition of national land ownership. In the meantime white squatters and a criminal element inclusive of all races poured into the countryside and created havoc.

Within 60 years what had been envisioned as a potential alternative by the Five Civilized Tribes, a land of their own, was taken from them and their future not only seemed bleak, it was. A last minute effort by the tribes to unite and form a "State of Sequoyah" was dismissed by Congress and the Indian Nations were combined with Oklahoma Territory and the 46th state was born.

For nearly a century after that the Civilized Tribes lacked the necessary financial resources to serve their people and struggled for the recognition of their sovereignty. But in 1988 passage of the Indian Regulatory Gaming Act has provided a new vista and, through a financial boon the Nations are reviving and offering services here-to-fore unimagined. The Pathfinders of the 19th Century would be proud of this resurgence. Now, only time will tell to what degree their original vision might be realized.

Personally, I have an immense curiosity about our forefathers and how they reacted to events in their lives. I looked forward each day to studying these men and attempting to encapsulate their stories. But in so doing it is also important to note that the development of Pathfinders has been a joint effort. While I have conducted the necessary research and developed the narrative, my wife Kay has reviewed each chapter amending grammar and revising punctuation as necessary. Additionally, it is also noteworthy to mention that much of the research and composition of the book has been developed with the aid of the computer. Consequently, a majority of illustrations have been provided by Google in addition to a few provided by the Oklahoma Historical Society or myself.

D. Bruce Howell, PhD

CHAPTER 1

The Land and Its People

A t first the quiet was interrupted only by the southern wind and occasional thunder storms in the summer and infrequent blizzards in the winter. Then centuries passed and large populations of gatherers, Caddoan speaking bands such as the Wichita, Waco and Taovaya, began farming the land seasonally. Perhaps because of drought, rivalries or a combination of both, the early settlers left but the land remained the same. To the west of the Grand River, first called the Ne-o-z-ho by the Osage, and later Six Bulls by French trappers, lay the Ozark plains and the Verdigris River named by the French. To the east of the river, first gently in the north but more pronounced in the south near the first community, La Saline (Salina) was the Ozark uplift, comprised first of hills then culminating further east as the Boston Mountains of Arkansas.

On early maps most of this region would eventually be designated as the Cherokee Nation and later Northeastern Oklahoma. Its wealth of natural resources that originally attracted aboriginal tribesmen later would become the territory claimed by Osage warriors. They would arrive following an ancient hunting trail, the Osage Trace, that is thought to have extended from present day St. Louis following the Missouri

1

River before turning south into the region. However, this land was only a small part of a vast expanse claimed by the Osage Tribe that ranged from the Missouri to the Red River and from the Mississippi to the Rocky Mountains. The Osage warriors were ideal guardians of the territory they claimed. Many were well over six foot tall, fierce and muscular men who fought many battles to protect their territory. Later arrivals would find them hard to dislodge.

The natural order that prevailed for centuries was eventually interrupted. In 1492 an explorer, Christopher Columbus, arrived from Europe and, thinking he had discovered a new route to India, labeled the inhabitants "Indians." The label was misguided considering the magnitude of tribes and the varied cultures, nomadic or place bound, that it encompassed. The singular label was akin to simply referring to all Europeans as "white," disregarding nations, boundaries or distinct cultures and their histories.

But even if the labeling of Native Americans as "Indian" was harmless, the eventual presence of Europeans flooding into this new world was not. In addition to occupying land claimed by Native Americans for centuries they introduced diseases that decimated tribes, new forms of religion through decidedly different forms of worship to the Great Father and violence through weaponry that killed from a distance. Theirs was a legacy that soon upset a balance of nature that had been known and understood since time began. Truly, North America was under attack and becoming a "new world."

Explorers and Early Settlers

Although Pathfinders begins with a category of documented early explorers in the region there are unfounded tales of the presence of white men long before. While it is known that

Francisco Coronado left Mexico City seeking cities of gold and explored as far north as today's central Kansas in 1541, discouraged with his quest he then returned to Mexico. But an interesting story from Osage tribal lore involves two men who allegedly strayed from Coronado's main column and ended up in far eastern Kansas. Captured near the headwaters of the Osage River, they were taken to the tribal chief, questioned, and after some time were released. The men then wandered on foot for over two years through the wilds of present day Missouri, Arkansas, Louisiana and Texas before miraculously reaching Mexico City.

Some contend that the first explorer of note to reach Northeastern Oklahoma was the Spanish conquistador Hernando de Soto. He is alleged to have ascended the Grand River but there is no evidence to support that. Rodrigo Ranjel, De Soto's personal secretary for the expedition, reported on events that occurred around present day Ozark, Arkansas, in the fall of 1541. He recorded two fierce battles with the Tula Indians east of today's Fort Smith, both won by the expedition, but noted nothing further west. At that point, according to Ranjel, the expedition turned southeast following the Arkansas River nearly to the Mississippi where de Soto died the following spring. Consequently, the first documented Caucasian is an explorer to what would become Northeastern Oklahoma, Frenchman Charles Claude Du Tisne. Du Tisne reached a small northern corner of the region in the early years of the 18th century. His mission was to determine the feasibility of developing a trade route and relations with the Spanish who founded Santa Fe a century before.

Du Tisne wasn't the first Frenchman in the region. Even though they are not personally documented, French place names like Verdigris, Poteau and La Saline indicate others were here long before. According to historical records unnamed trappers based at Arkansas Post had been trading with the Indians since its founding in 1686. Of medium height and physical composition, these were men who first came, studied and learned the way of the Indian, as well as how to dress, hunt and survive in the wilderness. To illustrate, centuries after they first appeared, Ralph Marcy[1] an army captain wrote a handbook for pioneers, *The Prairie Traveler*, describing the survival apparel needed for one man for a three month journey into the wilderness:

+ two blue or red flannel over shirts
+ one pair boots, for horsemen
+ two woolen undershirts
+ one pair shoes, for horsemen
+ two pairs thick cotton drawers
+ three towels
+ four pairs woolen socks
+ one poncho
+ four colored silk handkerchiefs
+ one broad-brimmed hat of soft felt
+ two pairs stout shoes, for footmen

Marcy also advised them to obtain repeating rifles and heavy duty revolvers for protection. "When not on the march, they should be placed in such a position that they can be seized at an instant's warning; and when moving about outside the camp the revolver should invariably be worn in the belt." Ominously, he also advised the reader to take a loaded weapon when bedding down.

The appearance of these early frontiersmen, the potential danger and their interaction with Indians or with some of their peers contradicted the romantic image held by some in the more socially sophisticated eastern states. Upon arriving at Chouteau's trading post at Three Forks, Washington Irving[2] who accompanied the entourage of Indian agent Henry Ellsworth in 1832 wrote, "Here was our escort awaiting our arrival; some were on horseback, some on foot, some seated on the trunks of fallen trees, some shooting at a mark. They were a heterogeneous crew; some in frock-coats made of green blankets; others in leathern hunting-shirts, but the most part in marvelously ill-cut garments, much the worse for wear, and evidently put on for rugged service." Later, when the Ellsworth party overtook a company of Rangers exploring the region west of Three Forks, Irving made similar remarks about their appearance, independence and indifference to authority.

Irving marveled at their survival skills. Stories regarding their resilience underscored their independence, their reliance only upon themselves. They lived in tents when hunting or exploring and some lived in rude huts when they returned to what loosely could be called civilization around the Three Forks. There were no written laws or moral code. A personal affront or cheating or stealing could result in death, and if the confrontation was deemed justifiable the matter was closed.

Violence was met with violence and traditional enemies gave no quarter. Osage warriors murdered and stole from the Western Cherokee for years before the Cherokee retaliated slaughtering old men and women and kidnapping others during a raid on an unprotected Osage village at Clermont Mound in 1817. Centuries of warfare were revisited when an Osage war party discovered an unprotected Kiowa village near present day Fort Sill in 1826, killing many and cutting off their heads.

Money or other valuables were either hidden on their person or buried in a secret place. Carolyn Foreman[3] relates an interview with the daughter of Nathan Boone upon his return home after several months:

> Then one fine day he would come tramping down the hillside hale and hearty…he would go into the bedroom and take off a concealed canvas belt on which had been sewed two canvas pockets…these pockets would be full of gold, for the government paid its soldiers in gold. Then the family would gather around while Mrs. Boone held her husband's hat upturned to catch the shining gold pieces as he counted them.

More often than not murders or suspects were not investigated unless there was some relationship to the victim. Grant

Foreman[4] quotes one incident that occurred in 1819 involving famed botanist Thomas Nuttall who may have narrowly escaped death at the hands of a frontiersman named James Childers, a participant in the murder of a Mr. Campbell owner of the Grand River Salt Works. Nuttall wrote, "At the Cadron, [a settlement] I had made application to Childers, one of these remorseless villains, as a woodsman and hunter, to accompany me for hire, only about a month before he had shot and barbarously scalped Mr. Campbell." Although Childers and his accomplices were apprehended, they soon escaped and were never hunted down and recaptured. Even 70 years later after some semblance of civilization permeated the region, the value of a human life had not significantly improved. Murders for trivial amounts or matters were still occurring despite the presence of laws and lawmen. Shirley[5] relates, "In 1888 William Walker killed Calvin Church for ten dollars and two bottles of whiskey."

Still, a few years after Joe Bogy established the first trading post at Three Forks in 1807, there began to be a counter to this vicious life style as more pioneer families filtered into the region and some semblance of order began to take root. The first "change agents" to arrive were missionaries, intent upon improving the lifestyle of inhabitants through education and attempting to convert them to Christianity. In 1820 Reverend Ephapras Chapman led a cadre of teachers, mechanics and farmers who developed Union Mission near the Grand River in today's Mayes County. When the Western Cherokee or "Old Settlers" moved from Arkansas in 1828, Dwight Mission, established near present day Centerville in Arkansas in 1820, was moved to its present location on Sallisaw Creek. The following year Dr. Marcus Palmer founded Fairfield Mission further north on Sallisaw Creek. God's emissaries had arrived and their influence both as ministers and educators aided in slowly, gradually improving the region's march toward civilization.

Women

There are no women on this particular list of Pathfinders because their influence and leadership essentially retreated then reappeared in the 20th century. The first three decades of the 19th century saw a heavy influx of male fur traders, hunters and soldiers into the region. Until the Western followed by the Eastern Cherokees arrived there was a comparative paucity of women pioneer settlers and their influence was marginal. Perdue[6] states, "Native American women exist in the historical shadows," and as far as it pertains to their impacting the frontier, the same observation also applies to Caucasian women during that era.

But the years preceding resettlement or removal were different. From its earliest known origins, the Cherokee society has been matrilineal and women were venerated for maintaining the existence of the tribe. Women farmed and controlled the fruits of their labor, they kept the household and raised the children. They were the center of tribal customs, the very reason for the existence of the village and in turn the Cherokee Nation. Men hunted and defended the village when necessary but women remained the life blood that provided continuity to the tribe. Their "bloodline" dominated and, day to day, they wielded considerable power. Some gained additional respect and decision-making authority being designated as "war women" or "beloved." But as the number of town councils decreased during the early 1800s that had an impact on the influence of women since town councils selected National Council representatives to discuss issues relevant to both men and women.

Missionaries were troubled by Cherokee traditions pertaining to marriage and the conflict undoubtedly impacted the number of female Christian converts and their social standing. It also had an affect on the total number attending church and school attendance reflected many more boys than girls. In 1830, again according to Perdue, Samuel Worcester reported in the *Cherokee Phoenix*, "that only 1,000 out of a total of 15,000 men

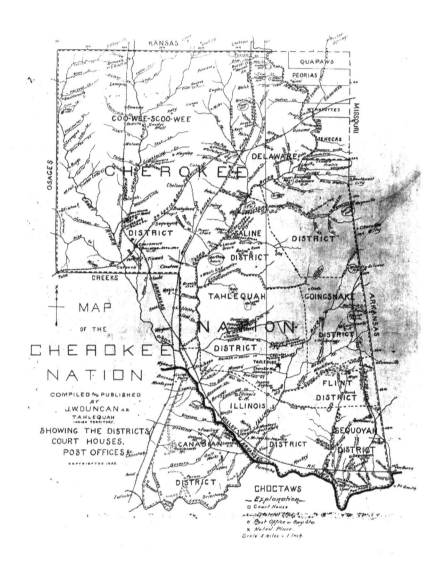

Courtesy of the Oklahoma Historial Society

Map of the Cherokee Nation

and women belonged to churches." The Cherokee wedding laws only required consent of the man and women in front of witnesses and the wedding ceremony could either be concluded at that point or become an elaborate event involving a variety of traditions. There apparently also was no limit to the number of wives a man could have as long as he could support them. Watt Christie, pathfinder Ned Christie's father, allegedly had eight wives. Those marriage customs existed until 1892 when the Cherokee Council passed more rigid laws defining marriage. There also were conflicts over the issue of infanticide which was an infrequent but accepted practice among the Cherokee prior to the influx of missionaries. However, the National Council eventually reacted to that situation when, in 1826 they declared it a crime and authorized 50 lashes for any woman found guilty.

Prior to the heavy influx of white traders, some women were recognized for contributions battling the enemy. The most well known in Cherokee history was Nancy Ward (Nanye'hi), when during a battle against the Creek Tribe, she lay behind a log to chew her husband Kingfisher's bullets so the ragged edges could do more damage. When Kingfisher was killed, Nancy singing a war song and using his rifle rallied the Cherokee warriors to victory. She was given the title "Ghigau" and became an ambassador and negotiator for the tribe. Beloved war women were given supreme power over captives and participated in the eagle dance celebrating victory over the enemy. During celebrations they were given food and drink ordinarily not given to other women. Over a lifetime that spanned 84 years Nanye'hi's leadership and council among the Eastern Cherokee became legend. Others, both men and women designated as beloved elders, were also selectively chosen for their wisdom and spiritual knowledge and given exceptional authority in certain tribal decisions.

These timeless traditions began to dissolve with the arrival of European traders when they began to intermarry with Cherokee women, bringing their frame of reference, domination by men, to the home. As these unions increased, this circumstance created a cultural division between full and mixed blood families within the tribe. To compound the issue, laws extended citizenship to children of intermarried Cherokee women, thus swelling their numbers. Full blood families attempted to maintain the life style of the past whereas mixed blood families adopted many European customs. Men negotiated with men, owned farms or plantations, bought slaves to till their land and acquired other European symbols of wealth and independence. The intermingling of races increased even more frequently after the Cherokee removed to Indian Territory. Whether for love or money, in order to legitimately acquire property it was necessary for Caucasian men to marry Cherokee women. But even then there were restrictions. As early as 1819, a law was passed forbidding white husbands of Cherokee women from disposing of any of her assets without her expressed consent.

In addition to being head of the household, Europeans were unaccustomed to dealing with women in matters of business, consequently Cherokee men, particularly mixed bloods, became more visible in tribal negotiations as Europeans sought to trade and treat with them. This combination of intermarriage and the focus on business caused a serious rift in what had been clearly delineated ancient customs that initially totally supported the matrilineal society of the Cherokee.

Although women, Caucasian or Indian, were cast in a supporting role most of the 19th century not all accepted that position. The wife of famed Deputy U.S. Marshal Heck Thomas tired of his long absences divorced him and returned to Georgia with their five children. Nor did they all maintain fidelity in their marriage. Annie Hitchcock, daughter of Cherokee Nation Judge L. W. Shirley plotted to have her husband killed by her lover James Craig. But Craig killed the wrong man, was captured and the plot exposed.

Following the early years of the 20th century Cherokee women generally began to reassert themselves in what had become a male dominated society. Women's suffrage, the right to vote, became a reality in Oklahoma in 1918 and nationally through the 19th Amendment in 1920. This is exemplified by Alice Mary Robertson, an educator and social worker who served in the United States Congress from 1921-23. Robertson, the granddaughter of Cherokee missionary Stephen Worcester provided a new image of leadership for women. Her accomplishment became the inspiration for other women who subsequently filled leadership positions within the Cherokee Nation. This was more recently demonstrated by the election of Wilma Mankiller as chief of the Cherokee Nation in 1985 and by Joyce Dugan who became chief of the Eastern Cherokee in 1995. So, after a temporary hiatus, It appears that the matrilineal values of the Cherokee Nation may have come full circle and the image of Ghigau is returning.

BIBLIOGRAPHY

[1] Marcy, Randolph B. *The Prairie Traveler*. Applewood Books. Bedford, MA. 1993. P. 39.

[2] Irving, Washington. *A Tour on the Prairies*. University of Oklahoma Press. Norman. 1956. P. 21.

[3] Foreman, Carolyn Thomas. *Nathan Boone, Trapper, Manufacturer, Surveyor, Militiaman, Legislator, Ranger and Dragoon*. Chronicles of Oklahoma, Volume 19, No. 4. December, 1941. P. 345.

[4] Foreman, Grant. *Pioneer Days in the Early Southwest*. University of Nebraska Press. Lincoln and London. 1994. P. 39

[5] Shirley, Glenn. *Law West of Fort Smith*. Eastern National. Fort Washington, PA. 2005. P. 225.

[6] Perdue, Theda. *Cherokee Women, Gender and Culture Change, 1700–1835*. University of Nebraska Press. Lincoln and London. 1998. P. 3. P. 171.

CHAPTER 2

The Explorers

The significance of the first pathfinder, French army officer Charles Claude Du Tisne, isn't that he was the first white man in the region. As noted earlier Hernando De Soto came close but his unsuccessful venture apparently discouraged other Spanish explorers whose primary interest in exploration was to find gold as they had done in South America. In 1541, the same year De Soto was approaching from the east, a Spanish counterpart, Francisco Coronado, was exploring the Panhandle of today's Oklahoma from the west and also seeking gold. After reaching what now is central Kansas, he too became discouraged and returned to Mexico. After Arkansas Post was established in the mid-1600s many anonymous French fur traders plied their trade in the Three Forks region but Du Tisne was the first Frenchman to officially be appointed to carry out a mission of discovery, a route to Santa Fe.

Simply by coincidence in September of 1719, the same year and month Du Tisne was exploring Northeastern Oklahoma, another Frenchman, Benard de la Harpe, arrived at a village of Tawakoni Indians on the Arkansas River near present day Jenks. The Tawakoni numbered about 6,000 according to de la Harpe.

His contact was made especially notable regarding his later report of cannibalism within the tribe. He recounts an incident in which the Tawakoni chief gave him a young Apache slave noting that we would have given him more but they had eaten 19. Apparently La Harpe's discovery of slavery and cannibalism among plains tribes wasn't unique as other traders and explorers encountered the same situations.

As a result of the failure of the Spanish expeditions to find gold, the region now became more influenced by Frenchmen who were fur trappers and traders interested in interacting with receptive Native American tribes. Besides Arkansas Post near the confluence of the Arkansas and Mississippi Rivers there has been a long standing debate among historians regarding a second French trading post in the future Oklahoma. Allegedly located on the Arkansas River near today's Ponca City, the post called Fernandina was said to have been established in the mid-1700s and was noted on a map produced by an English firm in 1856. However Wedel[1] discounts its existence after reviewing the questioning of French army deserters captured by the Spanish stating, "This raises questions as to why Frenchmen and Spaniards who were often glaring across their shared boundary at each other, why the French would name a post of theirs after the King of Spain." She offers further proof that a French post did not exist through the testimony of deserters and hunters who had been at the site in 1749-50. They did not refer to the name Fernandina at all. It is now generally agreed that at one time the site was an Indian camp where French traders following the Arkansas River may have been present from time to time to exchange wares for furs, as evidenced by a few artifacts that have been collected.

As in any successful trading arrangement each party possessed something the other wanted. Indians wanted guns, ammunition and cookware white Frenchmen wanted valuable pelts and furs to supply a growing market in Europe. This trade escalated considerably after Arkansas Post was founded. Frenchmen combed the region for furs and canoed up the Arkansas River where it joined major tributaries, the Grand and Verdigris rivers known as the Three Forks near today's Muskogee. Today as a reminder of the past French presence, several names remain. Foreman[2] notes, "The Poteau flows into the Arkansas…the word Poteau being French for post. The Sallisaw was named by the French as Salaison, from meat having been salted there…Cache creek, of course, is French." Verdigris was a French derivative for a greenish color perhaps because of decaying foliage or minerals that washed into the river. But there also is evidence that some places were given multiple names. The Neosho River, commonly referred to as the Grand River today when it reaches Northeastern Oklahoma is originally from an Osage term, Ne-oh-zo. But for unexplained reasons many French trappers called it the Six Bulls.

The significance of Du Tisne's exploration is that for centuries much of the region, later described as the Louisiana Purchase, had alternately been claimed by both France and Spain. In 1719, when it was controlled by France, the initial order to officially explore the territory was assigned to Du Tisne. His mission was to find a trade route with the Spanish to Santa Fe. Seventy seven years would elapse before Frenchman Jean Pierre Chouteau would follow Du Tisne, but in 1796 when it did occur, it was to expand the Chouteau brothers' fur business. The fur trade was enormously profitable. As a young man Jean joined his older brother Auguste in creating a virtual dynasty for their fur trading business in St. Louis, fed by western outposts and along the Missouri and Mississippi Rivers. But unforeseen events occurred regarding trading rights and now it was up to younger brother Jean to explore the feasibility of new fur trading territory in the southwest. Unfortunately after he arrived at his chosen destination, La Saline or Salina as we know it today, and establishing a camp on the Grand River he was confronted with a fundamental rule guiding any commercial business venture, location, location, location. After several futile attempts, he discovered there were no Indian villages within the necessary proximity of his trading camp, consequently no hunters to acquire furs. After returning with news of this dilemma and counseling with his brother, they arrived at a solution. The key to their conundrum would be attempting to persuade two Osage chiefs to move with their tribes to within general proximity of the trading post. This was accomplished and by the early years of 1800 two tribes, one led by War Chief Clermont, the other by Trading Chief Cashesegra, were resettled in separate villages about sixty miles apart along the Verdigris River. But within a short time the solution to their fur trading problem would create another when the Cherokee were relocated to what was then western Arkansas Territory.

The acquisition of the Louisiana Purchase in 1803 that included the future Northeastern Oklahoma would soon see the arrival in 1806 of American James Wilkinson who was tasked with exploring the Arkansas River from today's Great Bend, Kansas, to its confluence with the Mississippi. When his journey was complete, Wilkinson reported on the efficacy of building a fort for protection of settlers and constructing a factory (trading post) near the confluence of the Arkansas, Verdigris and Grand Rivers. Consequently all three of these men, Du Tisne, Chouteau and Wilkinson assumed useful but somewhat different agendas for becoming acquainted with the region. Although their objectives were diverse the reports and activities they engaged in laid the foundation for the first stages of the 19th Century development of the region.

Charles Claude Du Tisne

French officer Claude Du Tisne wiped the sweat from his brow as he and his Osage companion tromped through the blue stem grass west of present day Vinita. The head high grass and himself of medium height, Du Tisne could barely see where he was going and the September heat on the Osage Plains gave no sign of relief. This was the fourth day and 40 leagues or about one hundred miles since he had departed from the Osage camp north of present day Nevada, Missouri. But the distance and the danger seemed almost incidental since the Frenchman had traveled many miles and endured many hardships during his 31 years on earth.

Born in France in 1688, the son of Charles Claude Du Tisne and Catherine Duclos de Cursor, he joined the French Army and migrated to Canada in 1705. Married twice, Du Tisne had one son who was killed during the Indian Wars of 1736.

After spending several years at Quebec City, Canada, he was transferred to Mobile Bay, then in 1716, now as Lieutenant Du Tisne, he was placed in temporary command of the cantonment at Natchitoches in present day Louisiana. As a result of those experiences he acquired enough self assurance to know that now, with the advice of his Osage guide, he would make contact with the Panis village, if not today then tomorrow. Du Tisne volunteered for this mission, fully convinced that he could broker peace between the Panis and their arch enemies to the west, the Apaches. This would be the critical step in the French government's objective of establishing a trade route to the Spanish city of Santa Fe. Trade with the Mexican settlement of Santa Fe, founded over a century earlier, had been a long sought after objective of the French even though the two countries had squabbled for years over the prairie land in between.

The first key to obtaining this trade route was permission of the powerful Osage Tribe to grant passage through land they claimed. The Osage men, muscular and many between six and seven feet tall regarded their mission in life to be hunters, warriors and guardians of the vast western plains. Formidable in battle, they had laid claim to most of the land between the Mississippi and the Rocky Mountains for centuries. If a trade route was to be established positive negotiations with the Osage was an absolute necessity.

Still reminiscing on the past, as he trudged westward following the brief stint at Natchitoches, in 1718 Du Tisne was then ordered to the French village of Kaskaskia on the Mississippi River. His orders were to assist M. De Boisbrant, recently appointed as governor of Illinois Territory, where another cantonment along the Mississippi River, Fort de Chartres, would be constructed. It was from there that, earlier in the spring of 1719, with the approval of Governor Bienville, posted in New Orleans, he first attempted to reach the Osage by canoeing up the Mississippi River then west on the Missouri with a small contingent of men and trading goods. Unfortunately he was forced to return to Kaskaskia about half way through his journey when the Missouria Tribe, fearful of the Osage and the potential of their receiving French weapons, refused to let him continue.

Determined to fulfill his mission and make contact with the Osage, Du Tisne plotted a diagonal land route for about 250 miles, across the current state of Missouri that led him south of today's Rolla then northwest near the Lake of the Ozarks, and finally north of Nevada on the Osage River. There he located the Osage village which, described by Lewis[3] as, "about a hundred cabins and two hundred warriors. The Osages stay in their villages and spend the winters in chasing buffalo." He added, "Horses which they steal from the Panis can be bought from them." After arriving he contacted the tribal chiefs who, like the Missouria, were also fearful of his trading French weapons to tribes hostile to the Osage and refused passage.

An undocumented but interesting account persists about an incident that occurred while Du Tisne was in the Osage village that may have influenced them to change their minds. While bartering with the tribal chiefs instead of presenting his goods one at a time he made an amateur's mistake of laying out all of his wares. One chief turned to the others and suggested they just kill Du Tisne, scalp him and take his goods. Unaware that the Frenchman understood Osage, Du Tisne, who wore a wig as the result of a childhood illness, took off his hat, threw his wig on the floor and declared, "If it's my hair you want, there it is." Reluctantly, the startled chiefs gave permission for Du Tisne to proceed, but only with three guns, some trading goods and an Osage guide. However, unbeknown to him and still suspicious of his motives, they also sent a runner to the Panis in advance to spread the rumor that the Frenchman intended to enslave them and steal their horses.

Traveling southwest Du Tisne and his guide endured the hot September days that frequently occur. But almost as quickly as they had been swallowed up by the blue stem, they walked out of it and within sight of not one but two Panis Villages located near present day Chelsea, each with an estimated one thousand residents.

Suspicious of these intruders because of the forewarning by the Osage messenger, they threatened to kill them and it took time to allay the suspicions of the tribesman about their intentions. But it soon became rather obvious that the two were in no position to enslave the tribe, so discussions about the proposed travel route began.

Du Tisne was advised that Santa Fe was "30 sleeps" distant and he also learned that the Apaches, enemies of the Panis, were untrustworthy, highly unlikely to allow him to continue and would probably kill him. Recognizing those realities and discouraged by the distance as well as the time of year, September 27 which easily could place him en route during early upland snow, Du Tisne conceded that going further would be foolhardy. Instead, he planted a flag demonstrating French sovereignty over the land and negotiated the sale of his three weapons, the ammunition, pick axes and two knives for three horses and a mule. Noting the Spanish markings on the mule, he concluded that the beast had undoubtedly been stolen, coveted as the property of several Indian owners and that during its lifetime probably made the journey from Santa Fe that Du Tisne himself coveted.

Returning to the Osage village in early October and retracing his steps across Missouri to Kaskaskia on November 22, 1719,

Du Tisne sent a report denoting the details of his journey to Governor Bienville. Limited trade between the French and Spanish did not materialize until sometime later and it was not along the route Du Tisne anticipated, instead following the Arkansas River before turning southwest. For purposes of regional history the most important aspect of his journey was that it was the first official documentation pertaining to Northeastern Oklahoma.

Claude Du Tisne never returned to the region. After reaching Kaskaskia, he was assigned downstream on the Mississippi to Fort Rosalie near present day Natchez, Mississippi, and promoted to captain. In 1725 he was reassigned as commander of the second Fort de Chartres. The first, constructed in 1720 was washed away by Mississippi flood waters. He remained as commander at Fort de Chartres and died there on May 15, 1730 of complications resulting from a wound in the neck during a skirmish with Fox Indians the previous winter.

Jean Pierre Chouteau

On November 3, 1763, five year old Jean Pierre Chouteau, designated by future historians to become the "Father of Oklahoma," stepped off the Maxcent-Laclede barge and onto the dock at Fort de Chartres adjoining the Mississippi River. The barge, poled upstream from New Orleans by burly river men, contained trading goods that the firm intended to use to stock a trading post to be built further upstream in Illinois Territory. Jean was accompanied by his mother Marie, older brother Auguste and two younger sisters. Also aboard the barge was Pierre Laclede Liguest, a partner in the Maxcent-Laclede firm and rumored to be Marie's paramour, a subject within and about the Chouteau family that remains still much in debate.

The entourage had barely landed when Laclede learned that,

Jean Pierre Chouteau

under the terms of the Treaty of Paris ending the French and Indian War, the region then known as Illinois and other lands further north on the east side of the Mississippi had been ceded by the French to the British. Not to be thwarted, Liguest determined to simply move his trading post to the west side of the river on land still controlled by the French. After scouting a location some 35 miles north of Fort de Chartres he, with the assistance of 15 year old Auguste Chouteau, founded what would become the city of St. Louis. As it developed over the years, the original settlement on the river would approximate the 91 acres that currently constitutes the Jefferson National Expansion Memorial Park including the Gateway Arch.

As years passed, Auguste augmented by a relationship with Laclede in the fur trading business, became influential not only within St. Louis but also with the powerful Osage Tribe. When Laclede died on his boat near the mouth of the Arkansas River in 1778, Auguste invited his brother, 20 year old Jean, to become a partner in the firm. The business flourished to the extent that, by 1785 Jean, now married, constructed a spacious home for his growing family with grounds that covered a full square block. Through those early years the Chouteau family name virtually reached regal status in St. Louis and became well known to those founders further east who were busily engaged in political details regarding the recently formed United States.

Due to the vagaries of disagreements between the French and Spanish crowns, the territory known as Louisiana, south of the Ohio River and the vast expanse of what would become the Louisiana Purchase occasionally changed hands. Even when the Spanish government did control the region, the politically astute Chouteaus maintained good relations and a trading agreement with the Osage. They were sanctioned by Spanish Governor Baron de Carondolet headquartered in New Orleans. In 1794 Carondolet became concerned about the possibility of an invasion by the British from the north. Eager to curry favor with the governor, the Chouteau brothers volunteered to construct a fort at their own expense, on the south bank of the Osage River in what is now Vernon County, Missouri. However, a year after the fort was constructed, either his paranoia or tension subsided and the governor decided there was no threat of invasion so the brother's gratuitous effort was wasted. Even more disturbing to the two brothers was news that Carondelet had now granted the same Indian trading rights to a fellow Spaniard, fur trader Manuel Lisa.

Projecting that sharing a sanctioned trading agreement with the Osage within the designated region would dramatically reduce profits for their business the Chouteau brothers began exploring the feasibility of establishing trading posts further southwest. And so it was that during March of 1796, Jean Pierre Chouteau, accompanied by several Osage warriors and trappers, followed what was known as the "Osage Trace," an Indian trail west of St. Louis, to a river designated as the Ne-oz-ho by the Osage. In order to scout a location for a possible trading post, the men hollowed out a dugout from which Chouteau could obtain a better view of potential sites. He was seeking both access to the river and a place where there was gravel that would enable a passable ford across the river when it was low. While he floated down the river, the remainder of the party followed along the banks also comparing possible locations. Two days after launching the crude dugout he discovered the desired location, La Saline (Salina) so named because salt deposits were also found near the site. Salt would be necessary for curing the hides he hoped to obtain. Having found what he deemed the ideal site, Chouteau established camp and sent small contingents of men in every direction to contact Indians in the region who would be able to hunt and provide furs for trade.

If Baron Carondelet's approval for Manuel Lisa to also trade with the Osage was disturbing, the report of the various contingents of Chouteau's party who were seeking Indian hunters must have been a complete shock. One by one the parties returned with the same report, they found no villages, in fact hardly a trace of tribesmen in the region. There would be no viable trading post without hunters.

Discouraged but not defeated and returning to Fort Carondelet, then to St. Louis, Jean Chouteau concocted a scheme with his brother to move Osage Indian hunters within the proximity of La Saline. Having been involved with the Osage Tribe for over 20 years, they were fully aware of the mistrust, dislike and dissatisfaction among factions within the Osage Tribe. So during the fall of 1796, returning to the Osage villages, the brothers began a campaign to elevate issues within the tribe. Over time their successful political strategy ultimately resulted in two chiefs and their tribes moving to Northeastern Oklahoma. By 1804, Osage War Chief Clermont relocated his village approximately six miles northwest of today's Claremore near what is known as Clermont Mound. Osage Chief Cashesegra, known as the trading chief, moved his followers to the Verdigris River approximately six miles north of Muskogee. It has been estimated that combined, the two tribes may have numbered between two and three thousand. With the aid of politics and patience the Chouteaus now had their hunters.

But while the Chouteaus were engaged in reinventing their business through part-time tribal politics, an event of much greater significance was occurring. In 1803, France who laid claim to 828,000 square miles of land referenced as the Louisiana Purchase, including the region where the Chouteau's had negotiated, sold it to the United States.

The new owners took charge immediately, dispatching Meriwether Lewis and William Clark to lead an expedition in 1804 to explore the northwest portion of the region. And, because of his long standing involvement with the Osage, that same year Jean Chouteau was appointed as agent to the Osage and escorted Chief Pawhuska to Washington to meet with President Jefferson. Because of the combined oversight of his St. Louis business and duties as Indian agent, Jean Chouteau began making infrequent trips to La Saline, delegating responsibility to subordinates after it was reopened in 1802. In 1808 while continuing to fulfill his role as Osage agent he assisted in negotiating the Treaty of Fort Clark, convincing the tribe to cede lands in Missouri and the Arkansas River to the United States. Typical of most treaties with tribes, the conditions proved to be considerably one sided and later upset with the terms of the treaty, the Osage sided with the British in the war of 1812.

By this time Jean Chouteau was involved, not only as Indian agent, but he and Auguste formed an alliance with Manuel Lisa, combining their businesses as the Missouri Fur Company. Trading posts were developed that followed the Missouri River north to the Dakotas and several trading posts were opened in the region further south. As Jean Chouteau's business interests expanded he became less attentive to La Saline. Finally, in 1817, he turned the management of the trading post over to his son Auguste Pierre and became involved in civic and social activities in St. Louis. By 1820 the 62 year old essentially retired from the family business but he enjoyed a long and fruitful retirement. Jean Pierre Chouteau trader, politician and Indian agent died in 1849 at the age of 90.

James Biddle Wilkinson

While the Chouteau brothers were building a fur trading dynasty in St. Louis in 1783 another important event related to the exploration of Northeastern Oklahoma occurred, the birth of James Biddle Wilkinson to General James and Ann Biddle Wilkinson. The elder Wilkinson, handsome, glib and a Revolutionary War veteran, managed to amass an unenviable reputation both before and after the birth of their second son. Rising to prominence despite questionable political activities and during a lengthy military career, the elder Wilkinson seemed to be one of those with a gift for survival. The litany of shady events that comprise his life have frequently been described as Wilkinson being a general who never won a battle or lost a court martial. But, despite various indiscretions, the year 1805 found the resilient General James Wilkinson, Sr. as governor of the Louisiana Purchase. And, within that authority he ordered exploration of the greater southwest portion of the new acquired territory...again with an ulterior motive in mind. Although the Louisiana Territory was clearly the property of the United States, in 1804-05 the elder Wilkinson and a co-conspirator, former vice president Aaron Burr exchanged communications in a plot to set up an independent nation in the west. Exposed, the "Wilkinson luck" emerged again when blame was placed upon Burr and the wily Wilkinson was appointed governor of the newly acquired region by President Thomas Jefferson. In this capacity Wilkinson ordered first lieutenant Zebulon Pike on a mission to explore the west and southwest portion of the recently acquired region and befriend Indian tribes.

Wilkinson also ordered Pike to include his son on the venture although he had some misgivings. Earlier, the younger Wilkinson failed while leading an expedition up the Missouri when, after clashing with a band of Indians, the soldiers under his command rebelled and he was forced to return with them to Belle Fontaine, a fort and trading post north of St. Louis. Blackburn[4] quotes a portion of a letter from the general to Pike noting, "My son has the foundation of a good constitution but it must be tempered by degrees, do not push him beyond his capacities in hardship too suddenly. He will, I hope, attempt anything but let the stuff be hardened by degrees." As a consequence, James, Jr. was assigned what then appeared to be the less important task of exploring the Arkansas River from Great Bend in present day Kansas to its confluence with the Mississippi.

Pike departed from Fort Belle Fontaine on July 15, 1806. Included in the expedition were a surgeon, an interpreter, twenty one soldiers and fifty one Osage Indians. Traveling up the Missouri River they proceeded west across present day Kansas until reaching Great Bend. At that point Pike continued his western survey and Wilkinson, commanding a party of seven, would survey and map the Arkansas River from that point to the Mississippi.

Separating from Pike on October 28, Wilkinson expected to reach Arkansas Post near the mouth of the Arkansas in two weeks. Within hours of their departure came the first realization that the estimated two weeks would not be nearly sufficient. The group ran into shallow water forcing them to drag their canoes over sand and ice. Soon thereafter they were forced to abandon the canoes altogether and continue with what they could carry. As they proceeded their progress became slower and more dangerous. Freezing weather and the inconsistent depth of the river delayed them continually. By December 3, nearly five weeks after separating from Pike, the Wilkinson party had only reached the proximity of present day Ponca City. At this point they again attempted to float their supplies down the river but again the temperature fell below freezing, a snow storm developed and, chopping their way through ice, they alternately suffered from frost bite and exhaustion. Laboriously continuing their journey down the Arkansas past present day Tulsa, Wilkinson's contingent didn't arrive at the confluence of the Arkansas with the Verdigris and Grand Rivers until December 23, fifty four days after separating from Pike! The estimated two weeks journey, even to this point, had already almost turned into eight. Wilkinson's later report would dispel the possible use of the Arkansas as a suitable western waterway above the confluence of the rivers because of the inconsistency of the water flow.

Arriving at Osage Chief Cashesegra's camp on the Verdigris, Wilkinson delivered a message from President Jefferson pledging friendship with the Osage, pleasing the trading chief who wanted to negotiate with this representative of "the Great White Father." Blackburn continues by reporting, "Cashesegra, just as eager to reap the economic benefits of an alliance with his new white overlords, offered a section of land between the Verdigris and Grand River to be used as the location of a factory, or trading post." Later, in his report to superiors Wilkinson recommended that a fort be built on the land to establish a military presence, control hostile Indians and to protect future settlers and commercial ventures. Later, Fort Gibson would be located there. Unbeknown to Wilkinson the first commercial adventure, Joe Bogy's venture was being launched from Arkansas Post. Within two months the area would begin being developed and known as Three Forks, a site noted Oklahoma historian Grant Foreman would frequently refer to as "the cradle of Oklahoma."

Leaving Cashesegra's village on the Verdigris, Wilkinson's contingent moved downstream on the Arkansas now proceeding much more rapidly and passing the mouth of the Poteau River on New Year's Eve. Within nine days they reached Arkansas Post, 74 days or 10 ½ weeks after departing from Great Bend. Later when filing his report, Wilkinson noted incidentally that he had passed a French trader, Joseph Bogy or Baugis headed upstream with a substantial amount of trading goods.

Wilkinson's charge to map the Arkansas and surrounding topography and to make contact with the Osage was a success as was his meeting with Cashesegra. It established the initial foundation for both commercial development and military protection. In less than two decades, as settlers streamed into the frontier outpost now known as Three Forks, it would be a thriving business community protected by two Forts, Smith and Gibson. From 1807 until the founding of Kansas City 30 years later, Three Forks would be the major commercial center and departure point for the western frontier.

The ensuing years were not kind to Lieutenant Wilkinson. The hardships suffered from the Arkansas River journey apparently impaired his health and a few years later he refused the opportunity to lead an expedition west. James Biddle Wilkinson died in 1813 at the age of 30, his legacy of heroism and contributions were now secured.

Written history has not been so kind to his father. As usual, and despite his reputation for chicanery, at the end of his military career General James Wilkinson, Sr. managed to obtain a prestigious appointment, this time as ambassador to Mexico. But characteristically he became involved in still another scheme, this one involving a Texas land grant. While awaiting some resolution during the investigation of the details, he died in 1825 and is buried in Mexico City. In 1854 after retrieving the general's correspondence, a historian revealed many of his nefarious activities and since then others have supplied more details. In contrast to his son's legacy, the general's reputation has been verified and is also secure.

BIBLIOGRAPHY

[1]Wedel, Mildred Mott. *The Deer Creek Site, Oklahoma: A Wichita Village Sometimes Called Ferdinandina.* Oklahoma Historical Society. Series in Anthropology Number 5. Oklahoma City. 1981. P. 54.

[2]Foreman, Grant. *Pioneer Days in the Early Southwest.* University of Nebraska Press. Lincoln and London. 1994. P. 71.

[3]Lewis, Anna. *Du Tisne's Expedition into Oklahoma, 1719.* Chronicles of Oklahoma, Vol. 3, No. 4 Oklahoma Historical Society. Oklahoma City, OK. December, 1925. P. 321.

[4]Blackburn, Bob. *Frontier Adventurers, American Exploration in Oklahoma.* Oklahoma Historical Society. Oklahoma Historical Society. P. 8. P. 17.

CHAPTER 3

The Early Settlers

ollowing negotiations for the Louisiana Purchase in
1803, Arkansas Post, the settlement most responsible
for the fur trading that eventually materialized in the
Three Forks region, became the property of the United States. It
continued to maintain its importance to the region by becoming
the first capital of Arkansas Territory in 1813 and government
negotiations were often conducted there.

By 1804, shortly after Jean Chouteau re-established his
original trading camp and following several years of negotiation
the migration of the two Osage Tribes, led by Chiefs Clermont
and Cashesegra, was complete. Clermont, the war chief, chose
to locate the main village at what would become known as
Clermont Mound sixty miles north of Three Forks and six miles
northeast of present day Claremore. Cashesegra, the trading
chief propitiously moved much nearer to a location along the
Verdigris River and west of present day Okay. Although their
arrival would resolve an immediate problem of supply and
demand for the Chouteau brothers, it also initiated another,
frequent clashes between the new arrivals and other tribes,
particularly the Western Cherokee in what was known then as
Arkansas Territory.

As noted earlier, the Osage Warrior was inculcated from birth to either hunt or make war. And historically, the tribe laid claim to a huge portion of what recently had been defined as the Louisiana Purchase including the region around Three Forks. Although the Treaty of Fort Clark in 1808 resulted in the Osage deeding much of the land that is now northern Arkansas and southern Missouri to the United States, the terms, as usual, were either misunderstood or ignored. And now, typical of previous land deals, and following their own definition of the "Doctrine of Discovery," the supreme right of European migrants to own land in the new world, the United States Congress paid little attention to the feasibility of Osage claims. Because of this slight, the Osage who were long time allies with the French, their previous landlord's, joined the British against the Americans in the War of 1812. But now while they hunted to trade with the Chouteau's, the relocated Osage were also much closer and in a much better position to harass their old enemies the Quapaw and Western Cherokee, and they did. And white settlers were often caught in the middle.

During the summer of 1817, federal troops established a garrison at Belle Point, later called Fort Smith. However, Fort Smith was 60 miles, as the crow flies, from the growing community around the Three Forks and the intermittent clashes that continued between tribes proved the location to be ineffective. Recognizing the need for troops to respond more quickly, in 1824 the government established a second military presence, Cantonment Gibson, later Fort Gibson. The camp was located on the banks of the Grand River near its confluence with the Arkansas. Despite incidents between the Western Cherokee and the Osage continuing, eventually in 1825 Chief Clermont accepted a treaty with the United States promising to rejoin other Osage in Kansas. Clermont died in 1828 but the tribe fulfilled the promise, moving to Kansas in 1839, the same year most of the Eastern Band of Cherokee removed to Indian Territory from Georgia.

The Arkansas River that was such an enigma to James Wilkinson on his journey from the Great Bend in Kansas continued to be a navigation impediment to early settlement of the region beyond the Three Forks but occasionally even before. Rivers were the highways for commerce in the 19th century and although the addition of water from the Grand and Verdigris raised the water level in the Arkansas sometimes even that was not enough. While shallow draft keel boats, propelled by manpower and occasionally by sails, could navigate, it was a different matter when steamboats made the attempt. The first steamboat, the Robert Thompson, reached Fort Smith in the spring of 1822 during the flood season. As they plied the river from eastern river ports, attempts in the late summer and fall frequently left large boats stranded until an upstream surge arrived. To compound matters of navigation for a number of years there was a seven foot waterfall on the river between Fort Smith and Three Forks. It became known as Webber's Falls when Western Cherokee Walter Webber established a trading post near the river. Fortunately, for later river traffic the falls eventually eroded and disappeared. There also was a smaller one three miles from the mouth of the Verdigris that impeded upstream traffic on that river for a time.

For the most part until the mid-19th century, populated centers of business west of the Mississippi were almost non-existent although St. Louis, founded in 1764, was developing as a major business community as well as New Orleans and Cincinnati. Steamboats laden with supplies and passengers bound for the frontier began to arrive from those river ports with some regularity.

Despite clashes between humans and the impediments of nature, the settlement at Three Forks grew. Within two decades it was a bustling and well known center of commerce on the frontier and the surrounding region would remain in the forefront even after two disastrous floods would wash away the original site in 1833 and again in 1843. A settlement also emerged on the south side of the Verdigris across from Three Forks that remained and, with the development of Fort Gibson and the Creek Agency that soon would become Muskogee, the commercial status of the community was secure. In addition, from the early 1830s, when Mexico began admitting United States citizens to settle Texas, and even more so when Texas freed itself from Mexico in the revolution of 1836, the Texas Road that ran diagonally north to south across the region became a "super highway" for thousands of pioneers. A migration of a different sort, Texas cattle driven to northern markets on what would become known as the Shawnee Trail, would also impact the territory. While the Three Forks was developing as a commercial center, Francois Chouteau established a small trading post on the Missouri River that by 1833 grew into Westport, forerunner of Kansas City. The frontier of the Louisiana Purchase was inexorably marching west.

These were the circumstances and this was the environment enveloping those who came to this new frontier. As time passed, more and more pioneers occupied an expanding Three Forks region, some arriving voluntarily, others involuntarily. Comprised of a mixture of Native Americans displaced by force, joined by military soldiers, soldiers of fortune, and families attempting to become part of a better life, these settlers laid the foundation for what eventually would become Northeastern Oklahoma.

Joseph Bogy (Baugis)

There may be debate regarding whether or not Joseph Bogy should be considered an explorer or one of the first white settlers in the region but there is little doubt regarding his impact. After James Wilkinson departed from Cashesegra's camp, headed downstream for Arkansas Post in early January of 1807, he noted in his journal that he had encountered Bogy traveling upstream. Bogy and a small crew were poling a barge containing

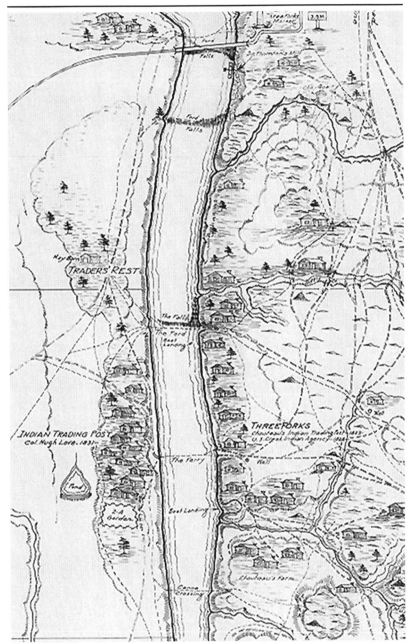

Courtesy of the Oklahoma Historical Society

Three Forks Trading Post

an estimated $9,000 worth of trade goods bound for Three Forks. As his background would indicate, the 55 year old Frenchman was there by design, not accident.

Joseph Bogy or Baugis was born April 13, 1752, in Beauport, Canada, descendant of a long line of French ancestors who first arrived in Quebec in 1641. Like his forefathers, Joseph became a fur trader and, at the age of 26, Bogy relocated to Kaskaskia, Illinois Territory. Shortly thereafter he married Marie Duplassy and the couple began raising their family.

In 1786 Bogy moved his family down river to Arkansas Post, establishing a trading post and continuing his occupation as a fur trapper. Undoubtedly it was during those years that he became familiar with the Three Forks area and conceived the idea of establishing a trading post. After the Chouteau brothers relocated Osage Tribes nearby, Joseph Bogy set his plan in motion.

The location he chose was southeast of present day Okay along the Verdigris River but as he and the crew unloaded the trading goods they were attacked by Choctaw tribesmen led by Chief Pushmataha. The Choctaw were at war with the Osage and the Chief, believing Bogy's supplies were for his enemies, confiscated all of them, putting a hold on the trader's aspirations. Unharmed but empty handed, Bogy and his crew returned to Arkansas Post where he filed a claim against the Choctaw chief under terms guaranteeing protection from theft in his trader's license filed with the United States government. Foreman[1] quotes a portion of Bogy's petition as well as a comment about Lieutenant Wilkinson:

> But sir, suppose the same Indians who fell upon me and plundered my property had fallen in with Lieutenant Wilkinson, whom I met a few days before, and not far from the place of depredation...suppose the same Indians, I say, had fallen upon him and his men...would the government have interfered in their behalf?

For years Bogy's petition languished in government red tape, even after Pushmataha, very popular with the government for his previous alliances with them, admitted stealing the merchandise. But the gears of government did grind slowly ahead and ironically five years after Bogy died, in 1836, the 26th United States Congress approved the petition, awarding $9,000 to his survivors. Despite his loss in January, during that same summer of 1807, Bogy returned to Three Forks, this time constructing a "Poteau style" log fort with vertical mud–chinked logs before supplying it with trade goods, then operating his business with a partner, William Drope, for the next two decades.

The settlement at Three Forks, inaugurated by Joseph Bogy, proved to be an instant success and Wilkinson's vision of the commercial potential of the area soon became a reality. The Arkansas, despite its fickle depth ranges, was the connecting link to civilization, at least to the Three Forks. While Wilkinson's report dispelled the idea of the upper Arkansas being a vehicle for commerce, below the confluence of the three rivers shallow draft steamers would be the link until the arrival of the railroad.

The population, in the proximity of the Three Forks settlement, was growing. In addition to the transplanted Osage, some Western Cherokees, Creeks and a growing number of white settlers and merchants were beginning to relocate there. The Brand and Barbour trading establishment opened in 1810. Others followed and by 1821 Hugh Glenn and Hugh Love arrived. In 1823 Auguste Chouteau, Jean's son who assumed management of the La Saline trading post, moved it to Three Forks and added a ship yard to construct huge barges. Thousands of pounds of furs, skins, bear oil, honey and beeswax were loaded on these barges and shipped to New Orleans. The government had not specifically established a "factory" or trading post as Cashesegra requested, but Bogy and other private enterprises made the request unnecessary.

But the government did fulfill another recommendation by establishing Cantonment Gibson along the lower reaches of the

Grand River and a few miles east of Three Forks. Pushed by the relocation of the Western Cherokee in 1828 and to protect the growing numbers of settlers and maintain peaceful relationships between tribes the cantonment, formally became Fort Gibson in 1832. Thus began a long and storied career that would see Fort Gibson become the most important military establishment on the frontier for many years.

Within this fairly short period of time Three Forks and the area around it also attracted the attention of prominent Americans. In 1819 famed botanist Thomas Nuttall spent several months cataloging plants in the region, on at least one occasion was accompanied by Joe Bogy. Later, an entourage led by Indian Commissioner Henry Ellsworth and included author Washington Irving would arrive and he would extol the merits of the region and encourage settlement in his publication *A Tour on the Prairies*.

In 1831, a year before Irving arrived, Joseph Bogy died at the age of 79. Perhaps it was fortunate because he didn't see his business destroyed by the devastating flood of 1833. Resilient, some merchants rebuilt on the prize location and others rebuilt on higher ground nearby. But time and location again were not in their favor. Within a decade another equally destructive flood destroyed businesses remaining at Three Forks and none were rebuilt. A century after it was founded there was scant evidence that it ever existed and today there is none. But, even though Three Forks has lost its physical identity the history remains. As Grant Foreman frequently reminds us it was a pioneer commercial venture that became "the cradle of Oklahoma."

Nathaniel Hale Pryor

Born in Amherst County in the Blue Ridge Mountains of West Virginia in 1875 and named in honor of the Revolutionary War hero Nathaniel Hale Pryor would establish himself as one of the elite founders of Northeastern Oklahoma. One of seven children, when he was eight years old his parents, John and Nancy, moved the family west to the falls of the Ohio River near present day Louisville. In 1798 he married Margaret Patton and a son Louis was born to the couple in 1800. Unfortunately Margaret died soon after and perhaps it was grief over her death that prompted Nathaniel to join an expedition to be led by Meriwether Lewis and William Clark in 1804 to explore the northwest portion of the recently purchased Louisiana Purchase.

Enlisting as a sergeant, Pryor was accompanied by Charles Floyd, a cousin who would gain the unenviable recognition of being the only fatality during the expedition. Sergeant Floyd died of peritonitis and is buried near today's Sioux City, Iowa. Pryor distinguished himself as a reliable soldier throughout the journey and received another important assignment after returning in 1806. When Lewis and Clark returned to St. Louis they were accompanied by the Chief of the Mandan Tribe, Sheheke and his family, who then traveled to Washington to visit President Thomas Jefferson. Upon the Chief's return to St. Louis in 1807, Pryor, now commissioned as an ensign in the army, was charged with assisting his return to the Dakotas. He was accompanied on this mission by Auguste P. Chouteau, with whom he would renew acquaintances several years later at Three Forks in Indian Territory. The expedition met near disaster in September when an attack by the Arikara Tribe resulted in several men being killed and the expedition turned back to St. Louis. The chief would not be safely returned until 1809.

Following the failed attempt, Pryor was commissioned 2nd lieutenant and appointed second in command to assist with the construction of Fort Madison, north of St. Louis along the Mississippi River in Iowa Territory. He resigned from the army in 1810 to start his own business, a trading post and lead smelting venture located further north near present day Dubuque, Iowa. However, two years later during the winter, his business was raided by Winnebago Indians who destroyed it and

Nathaniel Hale Pryor

held Pryor captive for a time. Miraculously he escaped, crossing the treacherous Mississippi on ice floes. Years later, under the guarantee of his trader's license, he sued the United States congress for repayment of his loss estimated at over $5,000. For unspecified reasons the suit was denied.

Following the beginning of the War of 1812, in 1813 Pryor re-enlisted in the army and, promoted to 1st lieutenant he was assigned to the 44th infantry. Later advanced to captain, Pryor served under General Andrew Jackson during the Battle of New Orleans and was discharged in June, 1815, when the army was being reduced in size during the post-war period.

Again attempting his hand at business, in 1817 Pryor purchased five acres of land at Arkansas Post to establish a fur trading business and formed a partnership with Samuel Richards. That same year he was married to Ashinga, daughter of Chief Cashesegra, the Osage trading chief who met with James Wilkinson in 1806. While the marriage was a success, the couple raised four children, Pryor and Richard's trading post was not. In 1819 according to a legal notice in the *Arkansas Gazette*, the firm was sued by its clerk for back pay and damages in the amount of $1,630. Other suits followed and once again managing a business was proving to not be Pryor's forte.

Fortunately for Nathaniel Pryor, it had been proven both on the Lewis and Clark expedition and as an officer during the recent war with Great Britain that he was skilled as both a woodsman and guide. During 1819 and while in Fort Smith, Pryor was approached by Reverend Epaphras Chapman of the United Foreign Missionary Society to assist him in locating a site for a mission to serve the Osage Tribe. After ascending the Grand River the men chose a site 45 miles north of the Three Forks that later became known as Union Mission, opening in 1820.

Having married Cashesegra's daughter, Pryor also became a trusted spokesman for the Osage and spent considerable time negotiating and representing the tribe when difficulties arose between them and other tribes or white settlers. He was appointed as temporary sub-agent to the Osage in 1827 rekindling ties with Auguste Chouteau who had also accompanied the Lewis and Clark expedition. Pryor traveled throughout the region to negotiate issues, frequently making trips to Fort Smith and to Cantonment Gibson. His success resolving disputes gained the respect of notables including Governor Izard of Arkansas, Colonel Matthew Arbuckle, commander at Fort Gibson and later, Sam Houston who moved to the area in 1829. On several occasions these men petitioned government sources to appoint Pryor as the full time sub-agent to the Osage. Foreman[2] quotes from one letter written July 3rd 1827 by Colonel Arbuckle to his superior:

> In relation to the pretentions of Capt. Pryor, I believe I am justified in saying that he has done more than all the agents employed in the Indian Department in restoring peace between the Indians on this frontier, particularly in restraining Clermont's Band of the Osages from depredating on the neighboring tribes, as well as on our citizens, which they had been in the habit of doing for a number of years.

Others wrote similar platitudes on his behalf but without immediate results.

In addition to his obvious skills in successfully negotiating differences between the Osage and others, his supporters had another motive…compensation for Pryor. His small trading post on Pryor Creek frequently became the target of angry tribesmen who resented his advocating for the Osage and they would steal his furs and other trade items. Consequently, the Pryor family continually experienced financial difficulties throughout the 1820s. While eventually his advocates did win approval of his appointment as sub-agent on May 7, 1831, and it was approved as a salaried position, there was scant time for celebration. After briefly being hospitalized for illness at Cantonment Gibson Pryor returned to his trading post on Pryor Creek. He died and was buried there June 10, 1831.

In 1982 during a military ceremony in his honor the remains of Captain Nathaniel Hale Pryor were reinterred at Graham Memorial Cemetery in Pryor, Oklahoma, the city that bears his name. In 2012 during a ceremony recognizing the bicentennial of the War of 1812, a marker noting his numerous accomplishments as a serviceman was unveiled on the lawn of the Mayes County Courthouse. Interestingly, no mention was made of his noteworthy contributions for nearly a decade as a peace-maker between warring factions during the settlement of Northeastern Oklahoma.

Auguste Pierre Chouteau

Although the Chouteau name is synonymous with the first settlement in Oklahoma, the result of Jean Pierre's founding of a trading post at La Saline (Salina), the family legacy was considerably strengthened by his son Auguste. Born in St. Louis May 9, 1786, to Jean Pierre and Pelagie Kiersereau, the indecisiveness of Auguste's earlier years gave little indication that he would become the Chouteau that contributed the most to Oklahoma history. In 1804 at the age of 18, he was appointed to the first class of cadets at West Point by President Thomas Jefferson. His appointment was made, possibly to curry favor with the prominent and influential Chouteau family. The recent purchase of the Louisiana Territory included St. Louis, now in the United States. Following his graduation in June of 1806 there were rumors of a Spanish invasion from Texas and he served briefly as an aid to General James Wilkinson. Whether he was disenchanted by his association with Wilkinson, who seemed to be the magnet for misdeeds, or was just discontented with army life he submitted his resignation the following January.

Perhaps in the spirit of adventure, during the summer of 1807,

Auguste Pierre Chouteau

Auguste and his brothers Pierre and Francois joined Nathaniel Pryor who was assigned to escort Mandan Chief Sheheke who had been visiting in Washington, now returning to North Dakota. But they were forced to retreat to St. Louis after several men were lost in a skirmish with the Arikaras, enemies of the chief and his tribe. Upon his return Auguste was employed in the family's St. Louis fur trading business until 1812 when the war with Britain began, and he joined the Missouri Territorial Militia, eventually being promoted to the rank of colonel.

During his years in St. Louis he was married to Sophie Labadiea and the couple were parents of six children. He seemed to settle into the routine of the family business, but following the conclusion of the war with Great Britain in 1815 he resigned his commission and entered into a trading partnership with Julius DeMun. They outfitted an expedition seeking furs and headed west following the Arkansas River that eventually led them to its headwaters near today's Leadville, Colorado, but in doing so they crossed into territory claimed by Spain. Both men were arrested and detained in Santa Fe for over six weeks and when they were released the furs they had accumulated, valued at over $30,000, were confiscated.

Returning to St. Louis, the future for Auguste Pierre Chouteau did not seem too promising. Now 31, he had resigned from a potential career in the army, and participated in two failed expeditions, but his fortunes were about to improve. What had become a struggling family business venture, the trading post located on the Grand River at La Saline, would become his salvation. As discussed previously, in 1796 his father, Jean, set up camp at La Saline with the intention of building a trading post. However, after weeks searching for Indian villages that would supply hunters and finding none he returned, convinced two Osage Tribes to move and hunt in 1802 and afterward the post became somewhat successful. But now in 1817 for a combination of reasons, including competition with Three Forks and conflicts between the Osage and other tribes, it was struggling.

In 1807 the Three Forks trading venture opened by Joe Bogy was 60 miles down river from La Saline. Since the business was near the confluence of the Arkansas, Verdigris and Grand Rivers it had a much greater potential for commercial success. Soon Bogy was joined by other traders, creating still more competition for La Saline. To complicate matters further, shortly after La Saline was reopened, in 1806 Auguste's father Jean Chouteau was appointed as an Indian agent to the Osage and was not able to devote the time necessary to manage the outpost or sufficiently capitalize on the earlier relationship he had forged with the two Osage chiefs. So, upon his return from Santa Fe in 1817, Auguste was assigned with the task of attempting to revive the business.

He entered into a partnership with Joseph Rivar, an experienced fur trader who moved to La Saline with his Osage wife to manage the day to day operation. Auguste remained in St. Louis, but occasionally visited the trading post. The partnership ran smoothly and Rivar seemingly formed a good relationship with the Indian hunters but in June 24, 1821, tragedy struck. Friction between the Cherokee and Osage had continued despite multiple efforts to appease both tribes and it occurred again when a war party of Western Cherokees led by Walter Webber killed both Rivar and his wife contending that he favored the Osage in trading negotiations. Without Rivar, Auguste was forced to leave his family in St. Louis and move to La Saline to operate the trading post himself. For the first time, and now left to his own devices, he began to develop the leadership skills that would define him for the future.

At age 35 and although he had not focused or remained in one vocation for long, that very circumstance would serve him in managing La Saline. He was seasoned in the life of the frontier, he had developed a wide range of personal contacts through his endeavors and he had become fluent in English, French, Spanish and several Indian languages. Following his arrival he took a second wife who was half Osage and supervised construction of a white washed two story home in the wilderness that would have been the envy of St. Louis. Importing valuable furniture for the home Chouteau also surrounded it with a lawn complete with rare shrubs and trees. All of these accoutrements were overseen by a staff of servants. And finally to complete the home surroundings a race track was also constructed.

Auguste Chouteau's home at La Saline became the center of society in this backwater region. In addition to local dignitaries, over the next several years he entertained numerous national icons of the era that included Sam Houston, Washington Irving, John Howard Payne, composer of *Home Sweet Home*, and a host of young officers from Fort Gibson who later would become household names during the Civil War.

But Chouteau's most important contributions to the early settlement of Oklahoma would involve trade and negotiations, not social activities. In 1822 he supported an expedition, that generally followed the Canadian River nearly to Santa Fe to open trade with the Spanish. Later, a similar route, the California Road would become a well beaten path to the west. In 1823 he bought out the Brand and Barbour trading operation at Three Forks and moved the La Saline trading post operation there. He also expanded the business by constructing a ship yard to build huge keelboats to ship commerce to New Orleans. For example, in 1824 his firm shipped over 38,000 pounds of furs, pelts and honey to the Crescent City.

While Chouteau was recognized as a successful businessman, he also became politically influential and, as settlers and trading expeditions moved further west he became instrumental in improving Indian relations. Known as "Colonel Chouteau," a result of his last promotion as an officer in the Missouri Territorial Militia in 1815, Auguste was called upon to assist in many endeavors. In 1832 he led a contingent, headed by Indian Commissioner Henry Ellsworth, that included Washington Irving from St. Louis to Fort Gibson on the old Osage Trace. Ellsworth was investigating problems with the Indian tribes.

Later, Irving published *A Tour on the Prairies* enthusiastically promoting the merits of the greater southwest and undoubtedly influencing many pioneers to resettled there. In 1834 Chouteau accompanied Colonel Henry Dodge to convince several Plains Indian tribes to send representatives to Fort Gibson for peace treaties. He also was aware that the fur trading industry was dwindling and began exchanging goods with plains Indians for their government annuities by constructing several western trading posts. In 1835 he established a trading post, Camp Holmes on the Canadian River south of present day Holdenville. He also built Chouteau's Post near present day Lexington in Cleveland County and another near Lawton in Comanche County. Mute evidence of Chouteau's presence in central and western Oklahoma remained long after his death. Marcy's travel guide printed in 1859[3] notes the location of a creek on the road from Fort Smith to Albuquerque as "Chouteau's Creek – Road passes on the high prairie opposite Chouteau's old trading-house...Excellent road, and good camps at short distances." The trading post near Lexington would also become significant. In 1850 Jesse Chisholm acquired the post located on the Fort Gibson to Santa Fe Road to supply 49ers headed to California seeking gold. Later, in 1866, the camp became a destination on the Chisholm Trail for trail hands herding cattle northbound from Texas to Abilene, Kansas.

Auguste continued in his role as businessman and entrepreneur assisting the government and military authorities when requested. Planning to return to the western trading posts the following spring, Auguste Pierre Chouteau died unexpectedly at his home in La Saline December 25, 1838, at the age of 53 and was buried at the Fort Gibson cemetery. Undoubtedly father Jean deserves the recognition that goes with the Chouteau name as the first to establish a settlement in Oklahoma. But it was his son Auguste who insured and expanded the family legacy through his numerous contributions related to the settlement of Oklahoma during the 19th century.

Samuel Houston

Sam Houston was unquestionably one of the most well known national figures to arrive in the young Cherokee Nation. His relationship with John Jolly, chief of the Western Cherokees, the first to settle in the designated region, and his political ties in Washington government circles brought visibility to the new nation.

Born in 1793 in Virginia's Shenandoah Valley and of Scotch-Irish descent, he was the son of Major Samuel Houston and Elizabeth Paxton. The major died when Sam was 14 and, shortly after, his mother and her family of eight children moved to Maryville in Eastern Tennessee. When he was 16, dissatisfied with working in his older brother's store, Sam left home to live with the Cherokee Indian Tribe although he still made periodic visits back to Maryville. While living with the tribe, Sam developed a close friendship with John Jolly. He was adopted into Jolly's family and given the Cherokee name Colonneh, meaning raven.

Sam's independence became further evident when, in 1812 he taught in a one room school house in order to pay bills incurred from his habit of constantly giving gifts to girls he dated. But his career as an educator was short-lived, when the Creek Civil War broke out he joined the Tennessee militia under command of General Andrew Jackson. The 6'2" Houston, unusually tall for that era, was promoted to 3rd lieutenant and when he was wounded at the Battle of Horseshoe Bend, his heroism came to the attention of the General. Thus began a lifelong friendship. Following the war, which ended in August of 1814, Jackson through his political connections, was able to have Houston appointed as Indian sub-agent during the early removal of some Cherokees from Tennessee to Arkansas.

Houston studied law and was appointed to the bar in 1818. Following in the political footsteps of his mentor Jackson, he was elected to two terms as congressional representative for

Samuel Houston

Tennessee. His success in the political arena continued and in 1827 he was elected governor of that state.

During his second term Houston married 19 year old Eliza Allen, a Nashville socialite but their relationship was short-lived. Reports vary, either she left him because he had sustained "a dreadful groin injury" during the Creek War or he drank too much. Other rumors suggested he left her because she was having an affair. Regardless, Houston resigned as governor, traveled to Indian Territory arriving on the steamboat *Facility* in the spring of 1829 to visit his old friend John Jolly, now Chief of the Western Cherokee.

For the next six months after arriving, Houston remained in a constant state of intoxication and became known locally as "the big drunk." However, this was about to change when he reunited with Diana Rogers Gentry, who he had known as a young girl back east. Earlier, Diana's husband David Gentry had been killed in Arkansas during one of the many conflicts between the Cherokee and Osage. Apparently Houston and Diana met at one of the many social events at Fort Gibson. Sam and Diana, the niece of John Jolly, were married in 1830 at the home of John Rogers on Spavinaw Creek.

The couple entertained numerous guests at their home and trading post called Wigwam Neosho, located three miles northwest of Fort Gibson on the Texas Road. The home was modest but the constant flow of visitors included such icons of the era as author Washington Irving, local businessman A. P. Chouteau as well as a host of military officers from Fort Gibson. Many travelers just passing through on the Texas Road also made the home a "must stop" to visit with the famous Houston.

In addition to entertaining, Houston became a representative of the Western Cherokees traveling to Washington numerous times attempting to seek resolution of details of the final treaty that caused their removal to Indian Territory. The city was familiar ground to him and President Jackson was a friend. In fact, during the course of negotiations other tribes frequently looked to him for support because of his influence. Locally, he also represented various citizens who were involved in land or money disputes, drawing up deeds and managing other legal details.

But the restless general and politician had other plans for his own future and they involved Texas, a territory he had long viewed as the land of opportunity. Gregory and Strickland[4] note, "Z. N. Morrell remembered a story told him by his friend McIntosh, a deacon of the Baptist church in Nashville, that Houston confided in the deacon a plan to renew his contacts with the Cherokees and, with their aid and assistance of his friends from Tennessee, 'to establish a little two horse republic' of which he would be the first president."

As events developed, Sam Houston accomplished even more. In 1833 he made the decision to leave the Cherokee Nation and go to Texas, but Diana refused to accompany him. He never returned to Wigwam Neosho nor saw Diana again. She died of pneumonia in 1838 and was buried at Wilson's Rock, rumored to be the place along the river that they parted.

Houston's predictions about Texas and his own aspirations seemed to verify his long standing vision and enthusiasm for its potential. After moving he led the Texas army to victory in the Battle of San Jacinto in 1836, served as its first president, and when it obtained statehood he was elected senator then governor. Although he ultimately reached his goals in Texas, apparently he also treasured memories and life among the Cherokee. During an interview in 1856 in Pittsburg, Pennsylvania, according to a news report W.W. Weaver[5] talked to him for several hours of the Cherokee Country and especially Talihina (Diana). "Mr. Weaver told General Houston of visiting Wilson's Rock and planting flowers on Talihina's grave. The General's countenance grew sad and tears filled his eyes. He said, there he spent the happiest days of his life." General Sam Houston, Cherokee citizen, president of Texas and twice governor, first in Tennessee then Texas, died July 26 1863 and is buried in Huntsville.

In just four years Sam Houston exerted considerable influence on behalf of the fledgling Cherokee Nation. Dislodged from a political career path in Tennessee that may well have found him as a candidate for the presidency, Houston sought comfort by rejoining his long time friends in Indian Territory. Inadvertently, his celebrity brought national attention to this region of the frontier. Fortunately his self-pity was short lived and the four years he spent with his adopted family provided both personal renewal and a period of contribution. His marriage to Diana became the catalyst, reviving the potential and self respect he was attempting to drown in whiskey. Once again he became competent, locally as a lawyer contributing advice and counsel to local citizens. Even more important, he gave the fledgling Cherokee Nation political visibility and credibility in Washington, a city he knew well. But possibly for those who focus on his relationship with Diana, if Sam had not followed his dream, instead of riding off to Texas while a tearful Diana supposedly waved goodbye, his additional contributions to the development of the fledgling Indian Nation might have further altered history.

Nathan Boone

There probably is no other pathfinder in the history of Northeastern Oklahoma with a more versatile personal history than Nathan Boone. He was a pioneer settler in Missouri, hunter, trapper, land surveyor, army officer, Indian fighter, constitutional convention delegate, fort commander and farmer. The youngest son of Daniel Boone seemed to "have it all." Born in 1781 to Boone and Rebecca Bryan at Boone's Station, Kentucky, the youngest of 14, Nathan was destined to have considerable influence on the new frontier created by the Louisiana Purchase.

Married in 1799 to Olive Van Bibber, that same year the young couple followed the rest of the Boone family to Missouri,

Nathan Boone

purchasing 680 acres of land north of St. Louis in St. Charles County and living in proximity to his father and several other family members. After subsisting in a cabin for several years, in 1813 he built a large stone house for his growing family that still stands today. Early on he supported the family as a hunter and trapper and, with his brother Daniel Morgan, manufactured salt in nearby Howard County at a site that became known as Boone's Lick. He was also employed by the government as a land surveyor.

In 1808, Nathan was appointed captain of a detachment of militia that ascended the Missouri River to attack the Osage, who had been harassing settlers, defeated them and assisted in erecting a trading post at a site east of present day Kansas City, first known as Fort Clark, then Fort Osage. At the time it was the furthermost western government outpost in the United States. A treaty was signed by the Osage ceding all land east of the fort in Missouri and Arkansas north of the Arkansas River. Returning to St. Louis, Boone was then ordered to lead troops in several skirmishes in Illinois during the Black Hawk War.

In 1814, the versatile Boone was hired to survey what became known as the "Boone's Lick Road" from St. Charles north of St. Louis west to Franklin, Missouri, a distance of over 100 miles. Later in 1821, pioneered by Becknell, the road was extended from Franklin through Independence to Santa Fe, New Mexico and became known as the Santa Fe Trail.

Now well known and respected for all of his endeavors, the 39 year old Boone was appointed as a delegate to the Missouri Constitutional Convention prior to its admission as a state in 1821. In 1832 as his introduction to what would become Northeastern Oklahoma, he was appointed captain of a regiment of Mounted Rangers and deployed to the newly commissioned Fort Gibson in Indian Territory. Recalled to St. Louis the following year, Boone assisted Colonel Henry Dodge in organizing and training a new division in the army, the United States Dragoons. It had been determined by Congress that a new unit, organized especially to patrol the new western frontier, was needed to maintain order. Recruited with much fanfare from all over the nation, these men, enticed by whatever needed to be said to persuade them to join and paid $8 a month, descended on Jefferson Barracks south of St. Louis. Following a summer of gaffes that included no uniforms, distribution of antiquated weapons and no horses, enough issues were resolved that finally by late fall of 1833, the troops left for Fort Gibson. After arriving and spending the winter, the inadequacy of their training, paralleled by the impracticality of their "parade ground" uniforms almost proved to be their undoing that summer. Led by Colonel Henry Dodge and with Captain Nathan Boone in charge of one company, the Dragoons left for the west with the objective of impressing plains Indians with the might of the United States Government. From the Dragoon's perspective, the mission was a disaster. Colonel Dodge and a number of troops died, others were left in small camps along the way, so sick they could not continue, and portions of the wool uniforms littered the trail. Both Boone and the remaining survivors were fortunate to survive, entirely as a result of the benevolence of the estimated 2,000 warriors with whom they did meet and confer...but did not impress.

Returning to Fort Gibson, in August Boone was ordered to southeastern Iowa to put down Indian uprisings there, then to command troops seeking to relocate Fort Des Moines from the Mississippi River to a more central location in the state, now the Iowa state capitol at Des Moines.

Returning to his role as a civil engineer, in 1837 Nathan was appointed to a three member commission to review the value of Fort Gibson as a frontier fort. The commissioners agreed that the fort should remain and also recommended construction of Fort Coffee, to be located on the Arkansas River upriver from Fort Smith as a deterrent to whiskey runners. He also participated in surveying a section of the Military Road from Fort Leavenworth to Fort Gibson that later extended north to Fort Snelling, Minnesota. In 1839 Boone served briefly as commander of the "New" Fort Wayne on Beattie's Prairie west of Maysville, Arkansas while troops constructed cabins and blockhouses on the site.

Called again to lead his regiment of Dragoons, for the next five years his troops were engaged in a variety of uprisings, ranging from southeastern Iowa to Fort Gibson, involving plains Indians who were harassing settlers as well as settlers fighting settlers. Boone also was obliged to resolve minor civil disputes. One involved his troops and Polly Spaniard, madam of a local house of prostitution near Fort Gibson. On March 11, 1845, two Dragoons were killed at the house and the following night it was burned by resentful soldiers. The dispute was eventually settled in court. In a more serious instance, the following December Boone and his troops were called to quell a possible uprising led by Stand Watie and his Treaty Party members against established Cherokee officials. Again, bloodshed was avoided.

Three years later in 1848, Nathan Boone was promoted to Lieutenant Colonel and, in that capacity periodically served as commander at Fort Gibson. The resilient son of the national icon, Daniel Boone, would continue to serve in the military until at age 72 in 1853 he resigned and retired to his farm near Ash Grove, Missouri. He died October 16, 1856.

Washington Irving

One of the best known of the Pathfinders selected for these biographies only spent a month in Indian Territory and just a few days in Northeastern Oklahoma. His name and fame preceded him. But perhaps more ironic is the fact that his appearance and his travels to this western most territory occurred purely by accident.

Washington Irving was born April 3, 1783, in New York City to William and Sarah Irving, Scottish-English immigrants. At

Washington Irving

the age of 19, Irving began his literary career by writing letters to the *New York Morning Chronicle*. His first major book, *A History of New York* published in 1809 was written under the pseudonym Diedrich Knickerbocker but his name became a household word later with the publication of *Rip Van Winkle* followed by *The Legend of Sleepy Hollow*.

Sailing to England after the war of 1812 to assist in rebuilding the family shipping business, Irving remained in Europe for 17 years and during that time his popularity as an author in America declined despite several publications. Returning to the United States in 1832, he developed a ship board friendship with an Englishman Charles Latrobe and his friend Albert-Alexander de Pourtales. Arriving in New York the three men decided to tour the Northeastern United States and the Great Lakes area together. During their travels they met Henry Ellsworth, recently appointed as Indian Commissioner, who was on his way to investigate issues with the tribes in Indian Territory. Ellsworth invited the men to join him and, after spending time in St. Louis they rejoined Ellsworth at Independence, Missouri on September 29, 1832, and, guided by Auguste Chouteau, 11 days later the party arrived at Fort Gibson.

Through the sheer coincidence of meeting Ellsworth and now, inspired by his new experiences in Indian Territory, in the next 30 days the talented 49 year old Irving would acquire the inspiration to reinvent the literary style that made him famous earlier. His journey supplied him with the wealth of material that would soon resonate with readers back east.

Leaving Fort Gibson on October 10, 1832, the Ellsworth entourage followed the Arkansas River to present day landmarks, first to Tulsa then west along the Cimarron to near Guthrie, then south and, by October 31st to Norman. Turning southeast they continued their journey through what was known as the "Cross Timbers" region, returning to Fort Gibson on November 9.

Irving painted a word picture of what he saw and what occurred that would make the most talented public relation's expert jealous. At the time there were few visual depictions of the region and virtually no written description by a seasoned author so his expertise as a wordsmith allowed the reader's imagination to become a far better substitute. Irving[6] described one fellow traveler that typifies his literary style. The camp handy man was represented as "a little swarthy, meager, French Creole, named Antoine, but familiarly dubbed Tonish; a kind of Gil Blas of the frontiers, who had passed a scrambling life, sometimes among white men, sometimes among Indians; sometimes in the employee of traders, missionaries and Indian agents; sometimes mingling with the Osage hunters." He described others in the party in the same finite terms that gave the reader a sense of actually being a part of the entourage. No one escaped mention including a description of an Indian hunter on the prairie who "Like a cruiser on the ocean, perfectly independent of the world, and competent to self-protection and self-maintenance. He can cast himself loose from everyone, shape his own course, and take care of his own fortunes."

Having made the reader familiar with some of the traveling companions Irving then describes a care free life where decisions to hunt or deviate from yesterdays plan are commonplace. Members of the party hunt, chase buffalo and ride through forests streaming with sunlight reminding Irving of "the effect of sunshine among stained windows and clustered columns of a Gothic cathedral." He describes "The beautiful forest in which we were encamped abounded in bee-trees; that is to say trees in the decayed trunks of which wild bees had established their hives." And after extolling the beauty of the region Irving invokes the biblical reference of "a land of milk and honey." He describes the beauty of the journey relaxing at one encampment, "For my own part, I lay on the grass under the trees, and built castles in the clouds, and indulged in the very luxury of rural repose." His choice of words and descriptive phrases would become persuasive enough to entice many adventurers to take advantage of the potential and free life style on the frontier.

Irving returned east continuing to refine the details of his journal and completed it during November of 1834. In March, 1835, *A Tour on the Prairies* was published in London recapturing his popularity and status among American authors. For the next several years he continued writing on themes about the west following *A Tour of the Prairies* with best sellers *Astoria* and the *Adventures of Captain Bonneville*. His legacy as one of America's premier authors once more secure, Washington Irving died November 28, 1859 and fittingly is buried in the Sleepy Hollow Cemetery, Sleepy Hollow, New York.

The impact of Irving's brief tour on the edge of the western frontier and his publication cannot be measured directly on how it impacted the public's attitude toward this new frontier. But almost simultaneously following the publication of *A Tour on the Prairies* the land rush to Texas began with thousands of travelers using the Texas Road through Northeastern Oklahoma. There had been numerous military reports and some articles reflecting information about the frontier, but none that would describe the region to the reading public with Irving's flair for composition. His writing captured the beauty, potential and romance of adventure that undoubtedly became the inspiration for many pioneers to take the risk and come to the country that he paraphrased as being "a land of milk and honey."

BIBLIOGRAPHY

[1]Foreman, Grant. *Pioneer Days in the Early Southwest.* University of Nebraska Press. Lincoln and London. 1944. P. 73.

[2]Foreman, Grant. *Nathaniel Pryor.* Chronicles of Oklahoma. Volume 7, No. 2. June, 1929. P. 162.

[3]Marcy, Randolph B. *The Prairie Traveler.* Applewood Books. Bedford, MA. 1859. Appendix: List of Itineraries.

[4]Gregory, Jack and Strickland, Rennard. *Sam Houston with the Cherokees, 1828 –1833.* University of Oklahoma Press. Norman. 1967. P. 141.

[5]Wilson, William. *Talihina's Grave.* The Fort Gibson Post. July 21, 1904.

[6]Irving, Washington. Edited by John Francis McDermott. *A Tour on the Prairies.* University of Oklahoma Press. Norman. 1956. P. 28, P. 41, P. 51, P. 85.

CHAPTER 4

Cherokee Transitional Leaders

The next category of Pathfinders are men with roots in their Cherokee heritage who played prominent roles in the developing storm that eventually led to the tribe transitioning to Indian Territory. Their early efforts for conciliation to prevent removal only delayed the inevitable. Despite several aligning themselves with troops under the command of Andrew Jackson during the Creek and Seminole Wars in 1813-14, that association did nothing to sway Jackson's personal opinion regarding removal.

In 1827, modeling their own government to that of the United States, the Cherokees sought to use arguments framed in debate similar to that of congress. When asked his opinion regarding the progress toward assimilation of Indians during the last eight years, in compliance with a resolution from the United States Senate, Reverend Samuel Worcester[1] responded with a detailed and highly positive letter:

> By all these remarks I do not intend to convey the impression, that the Cherokees have already reached, or nearly reached a level with the white people of the United States in point of civilization. But they made great advances, and are steadily advancing still...Any

theory in regard to their removal from this place, which is built upon the supposition of the impossibility of their rising where they are, is opposed to fact. They can rise for they are rising.

But even after winning several court rulings including a major victory in the Supreme Court, *Worcester v. Georgia* in 1832, their quest for sovereignty was still ultimately ignored by federal officials. By this time, emboldened by the actions of President Jackson to remove the Cherokee, the state of Georgia ordered Cherokee land be surveyed, divided into 160 acre allotments and auctioned off to prospective white settlers.

Some tribesmen had seen the proverbial "handwriting on the wall," much earlier. Several decades before their ultimate expulsion in 1839, Cherokee began migrating west from the Georgia/Tennessee region, crossing the Mississippi and relocating in the eastern portion of today's Missouri and Arkansas. Now as white settlers began infringing on the Cherokee Nation East and mixed blood marriages became more prevalent, more bowed to the inevitable. Relocated, these Western Cherokee were able to resume the traditional lifestyle they wished to maintain, and extolled the virtues of living there to their eastern counterparts. However, in 1817 as the result of a disputed treaty with the United States regarding exchanging territory in eastern Arkansas for land further west, they were forced to move again with most settling near the Arkansas River from today's Johnson County on west to the mouth of the Poteau River. But for the first time, the explicit boundaries reflected in the new treaty did give Chief Tahlonteskee and the Western Cherokee a designated territory, one approved by the United States government.

The relocation only heightened tensions between the Cherokee and the Osage who despite the treaty of Fort Osage in 1808 still claimed land south from the Missouri River to the Arkansas. Unfortunately, the new treaty moved the villages of the two tribes even closer together. Ever since the arrival of the Western Cherokee late in the 18th century, violence had sporadically erupted with the Osage. Authorities frequently sought resolutions to these bitter conflicts. Nearly ten years after the arrival of the first permanent white residents around the Three Forks, in June of 1816 Indian sub-agent William Lovely negotiated what appeared to be an agreement on his own with approval for a "buffer zone" between the two factions. The agreement dubbed "Lovely's Purchase" involved seven million acres ranging from the Verdigris River eastward beyond the present western border of Arkansas, however the agreement had not been approved by the government and wouldn't for several years.

It was not very effective. Almost immediately numerous incidents incited by the Osage occurred in violation of the "buffer zone." As a result according to Foreman[2], Tahlonteskee and other Cherokee chiefs wrote to Governor Clark:

> ...that for nine years they had been trying to make friends with the Osage, but to no purpose; that they had been trying to raise crops for their families but the Osage had stolen their horses so that they were reduced to working the land with their bare hands; they had promised the President not to spill the blood of the Osage if they could help it, but that now the rivers were running with the blood of the Cherokee, they had determined to proceed against their enemies.

And they did. To counter these intrusions the Western Cherokee developed a plan of retribution with the objective of annihilating Clermont and the Osage war chief's village by organizing a coalition of local tribes and white settlers. Lead by Cherokee War Chief Degadoga and leaving the territory near today's Clarksville, Arkansas, and following the Arkansas then Verdigris Rivers, over 500 warriors reached Clermont's village in late October of 1817 and attempted to do just that. However, the attack did not materialize as planned. Clermont and most of the able bodied Osage warriors were not in camp, engaged instead in a fall buffalo hunt further west. The coalition attacked the village anyway and the result was the slaughter of over 80 camp occupants, primarily the elderly, and kidnapping women and children. Although conflicts between the factions did not stop entirely the massacre marked the beginning of the end of Osage dominance in the region. In the meantime, Cherokee migrants from Georgia and Tennessee continued to arrive in western Arkansas Territory, among them the brother of Tahlonteskee, John Jolly.

John Jolly (Ahuludegi)

John Jolly is first introduced in history as headman of a Cayuga town on Hiwassee Island frequently referred to as "Jolly's Island," in Tennessee. Little is known of his early years but, as time passed, he became a wealthy merchant and a leader among the plantation element of the Cherokee and, like the rest, owned numerous slaves. Gregory and Strickland[3] quote the famous painter George Catlin who described Jolly as "a dignified chief... a mixture of white and red blood, of which...the first seems decidedly to predominate." But at the time, the most relevant aspect of Jolly's years on Hiwassee Island involving the future was a friendship developed with Sam Houston. Houston ran away from home at the age of 16 because of a disagreement with an older brother and came to live on Hiwassee Island. Almost immediately, Jolly and Houston bonded and the chief adopted him into the tribe.

In February of 1818, Jolly and his family, along with a contingent of 300 other tribesmen, relocated to west central Arkansas near present day Clarksville reuniting with his brother, Chief Tahlonteskee. Earlier, in 1807, the Chief and his followers moved to Arkansas following the conclusion of the Louisiana Purchase. Then, as a result of a contested treaty in 1817, the Western Cherokee moved further west. Concerned about the education of the young, Tahlonteskee returned to Georgia and

John Jolly

persuaded Reverend Cephas Washburn to establish what would become the original Dwight Mission in 1820 near Clarksville. John Jolly was instrumental in aiding in its development.

The chief died in the spring of 1819 and Jolly was elected civil chief to oversee internal affairs and for diplomacy with United States government officials. Later, during a reorganization of their government, in 1824 he was chosen president of the tribal council. Once again the boundaries of Western Cherokee lands were in dispute because the government now wanted to create the territory of Arkansas into a state and move the tribe even further west into the region now designated as "Indian Territory." As President Jolly worked tirelessly to dissuade the federal government in 1828 the tribe reluctantly agreed. They gave up their lands and moved further west into what is now Oklahoma. The United States, having once again successfully abrogated an Indian treaty, admitted Arkansas to the Union in 1836 as a slave state.

Jolly relocated his plantation near the confluence of the Illinois and Arkansas rivers and continued with the details of governing the Western Cherokees at the site of the new government, Tahlonteskee. The site was located near the mouth of the Illinois River near present day Gore. Soon afterward, in the spring of 1829, he was reunited with his friend and adopted son, Sam Houston. Chief Jolly along with Houston, his political advisor, and John Rogers, his brother-in-law, worked closely to develop the ground rules for the fledgling nation and they all spent considerable time negotiating in Washington. During his tenure as chief of the Western Cherokee the new nation adopted a constitution and developed a tripartite government.

Government agents in the east were able to persuade a limited number of Eastern Cherokee to move west on barges and steamboats. Their assimilation into the "new Indian Territory" proved to be challenging for the fledgling Western Cherokee government. They did not welcome these new migrants because, as frequently occurred, United States government promises of food and money went unfulfilled placing a strain on their own resources. Eventually, Jolly and his associates were able to negotiate a treaty that would increase annuities and land holdings for current residents and a limited number of arrivals were accepted. However, later when the Eastern Cherokee were relocated, divisions again emerged between the newcomers and the "Old Settlers" that would resonate for years.

John Jolly was the first chief of the new Cherokee Nation and played an outstanding role in assisting its initial transition into Indian Territory. His leadership of the Western Cherokee and the formation of that first government laid a foundation for the larger body of Eastern Cherokee who moved in 1839. Following his arrival in Arkansas in 1818, he was immediately cast in important leadership positions, first as Civil Chief, then Council President and finally as Chief of the Western Cherokee. Assistance in the developmental stages of this new nation also occurred with Jolly's longstanding relationship with Sam Houston. Houston, with his knowledge of Washington politics, contributed valuable advice and assistance to Jolly. From 1828 until 1838 after the relocation of John Ross and his Eastern Cherokee administration, Jolly's "Old Settler" government allowed time for the fledgling nation to become established. Eventually, although reluctantly, under Ross' leadership the transition was accomplished and by the mid-1840s a united nation emerged.

Elias Boudinot (Gallegina Uwati)

Born in Georgia in 1802, Gallegina Uwati was the eldest son of Uwati and Susanna Reese of mixed blood. He had two younger brothers, Stand and Thomas. At the age of six he attended the Moravian Missionary School and after the foreign missions board opened a school in Cornwall, Connecticut in 1817 he was invited to enroll. During his journey to Cornwall, Uwati met Elias Boudinot, president of the American Bible Society and

Elias Boudinot

the two immediately bonded. Impressed with Boudinot, young Uwati requested permission to use the president's full name which he kept for the remainder of his life.

In 1824 he assisted in translating the New Testament into the Cherokee language developed by Sequoyah. Two years later, Boudinot married Harriet Gold, the member of a prominent Connecticut family and they moved to Georgia. The couple had six children before Harriet tragically died from complications resulting from the birth of the seventh child in 1836.

In 1828, Boudinot was selected by the General Council of the Cherokee Nation as editor of the first newspaper to be published by a Native American nation, the *Cherokee Phoenix*. Collaborating with Samuel Worcester, a white missionary, the two printed the paper in both Cherokee and English. The *Phoenix* focused primarily on publishing new laws, political information, and editorials composed by Boudinot. But most important, with the new syllabary developed by Sequoyah, it provided a new source of communication for the tribe.

For the next four years his editorials in the *Phoenix* increasingly railed against activities by both the state of Georgia and the federal government and their efforts to confiscate Cherokee land and promote removal to Indian Territory. The governmental pressure for removal increased substantially after gold was discovered in northwest Georgia in 1829.

Following passage of the 1830 Indian Removal Act by the United States Congress, reactions among Cherokee tribesmen were divided. The majority led by Chief John Ross opposed the act, convinced that a settlement could be reached that would enable the tribe to remain on their native land. A minority also opposed the act but believed removal was inevitable and favored negotiating a pact, among them Elias Boudinot, whose editorials not only promoted negotiations but criticized Ross and the Cherokee National Party for their intractable position. Because of the disagreement, Boudinot resigned as editor in 1832 and within two years the paper ceased publication under pressure both from the state of Georgia as well as the National Party for advocating for a treaty with the government

Determined to rid themselves of the Cherokee, white Georgians increased personal harassment of the tribesmen and the Georgia legislature passed oppressive and unreasonable laws focused on the Indians. These actions led the Cherokee minority, now referred to as the "Treaty Party," to become even more convinced that a removal settlement was needed. As a result, secret negotiations began with both Georgia and federal authorities. In Washington the climate related to the acceptance of this minority was evident. Treaty Party representatives were welcomed during discussions of the issue while delegations from the National Party, led by Ross, were virtually ignored. Negotiations between the Treaty Party delegation and the federal government officials progressed to the point that, despite having no approval by either the Cherokee government or a vast majority of the population, an agreement dubbed the Treaty of New Echota, was authorized. On December 29, 1835, twenty Cherokee cosigners, including Elias Boudinot, signed the treaty. This was all advocates in Washington needed to press removal and it was ratified by the United States Senate the following March. But there was evidently concern within the members of the senate regarding this approval by so few Cherokee and the ratification passed by only one vote.

As could be expected, the animosity toward the signers and their families forced most to move to Indian Territory and they joined the Western Cherokee who in 1828 had inaugurated the new Cherokee Nation. In 1836 Elias Boudinot relocated to Park Hill, built a home, was reunited with his friend Samuel Worcester, and the two resumed their efforts to translate and print the New Testament into the Cherokee language. Boudinot also remarried shortly after coming to Park Hill and seemingly had settled into a routine scholarly life in his adopted nation, but fate dictated otherwise. On June 22, 1839, following the arrival of Eastern Cherokee and the disastrous Trail of Tears, a well orchestrated assassination plot claimed his life and two of his fellow treaty cosigners. Their deaths signaled the beginning of over a decade of violence between the two factions.

Elias Boudinot became a popular figurehead for those resigned to removal and a flash point for those against it. He rose to prominence when in 1824 he assisted in translating the New Testament into the Cherokee language created by Sequoyah. Boudinot's influence in the Nation increased substantially when he was selected as the first editor of the *Cherokee Phoenix*. He used the position in the early years to oppose removal, however upon learning that the U.S. Supreme Court had ruled in favor of the Cherokees in *Worcester v. Georgia* and that President Andrew Jackson ignored the ruling, Boudinot began advocating for terms of a peaceful resolution in his editorials. His articles, as well as criticism of Chief John Ross, finally forced his resignation from the *Phoenix* in 1832. By this time he had been cast in a leadership role as a member of the "Treaty Party," and, in fact did sign the treaty in 1835. His assassination and others that took place following the Cherokee removal signaled the beginning of a horrific division within the Nation that, on occasion, still resonates today.

Major Ridge (Kah-numg-da-cla-gah)

Believed to have been born in 1771, the son of a Scots-Cherokee mother and a Cherokee father, The Ridge or *Kah-Numg-da-cla-Gah*, meaning "The Man Who Walks On The Mountain Top" became a respected warrior and Cherokee patriot. During his early years he participated in numerous successful raids against white settlers, but also developed a personal feud with Cherokee Chief Doublehead. Through the years Doublehead acquired a reputation for murder, cannibalism and corruption. In one instance known as the massacre at Cavett's Station, a family consisting of three men, ten women and

Major Ridge

several children barricaded themselves in a blockhouse because they were hopelessly outnumbered by a war party. When the leader promised to spare their lives and they opened the door, Doublehead rushed in killing 12 of the 13 family members. In another, Doublehead and two cohorts ambushed two Americans, scalped them then roasted their flesh and ate it. Because of these and numerous other atrocities and misdeeds, Ridge became his avowed enemy. In 1807 when Doublehead engaged in some illegal land sales, the Cherokee leadership had enough and the Cherokee National Council gave approval for Ridge and James Vann to track down and kill the old renegade.

In 1792, a year before the Cavett massacre, Ridge married Suzannah Wickett, a mixed blood Cherokee and that same year at the age of 21 was chosen as a member of the Cherokee Council. The couple had several children and lived near today's Calhoun, Georgia. Sixteen years later they would move to a site near modern day Rome, Georgia, where Ridge developed a 300 acre plantation near the Oostanuaula River assisted by 30 slaves. He also owned a profitable trading post and ferry.

The Cherokee, who actually fought alongside the British in the Revolutionary War, sided with the United States when it became involved in a civil war between two factions within the Creek Nation. Troops consisting of state militia, as well as Cherokee and Lower Creek tribesmen were led to victory at the Battle of Horseshoe Bend by Andrew Jackson. Because of his heroism, Ridge was promoted to Major by Jackson, a title he continued to use for the remainder of his life.

However, this would not be Ridge's or the Cherokee Nation's last encounter with Andrew Jackson. By 1815 Jackson had acquired a distinguished career in the military resulting primarily from his successful defeat of the British during the Battle of New Orleans. The feat propelled him into politics. Following a successful career in state and national politics, he ran for president twice and was elected by a landslide the second time in 1828. But his election did not bode well for his Cherokee acquaintances' or other tribes because Jackson immediately began pressing for Indian removal to land acquired through the Louisiana Purchase. The issue became particularly acute in the southeastern portion of the United States where Indian population, particularly the Cherokees, many of whom had assimilated into the white man's customs, were occupying land that impeded white settlement. When the issue of Cherokee removal became a constant topic Ridge initially opposed it. But as time passed and oppressive laws were passed by the Georgia legislature in the 1820s he began to change his mind. Following discussions with his son John Ridge who was clerk of the National Council, Major Ridge slowly came to terms with the concept.

Meanwhile, both the National Party and the Cherokee National Council, who represented the vast majority of Cherokee tribesmen, remained strongly opposed. While the National Party continued to lobby Congress to prevent removal, a splinter group now identified as the "Treaty Party" pressed for a removal pact. It was their belief that it was inevitable and some compensation for the land, coupled with expenses to cover the journey, was better than simply being forced to leave. As noted previously, tensions increased when both factions visited in Washington. Treaty Party members were feted while those from the National Party were virtually ignored. Meanwhile, mirroring the climate of rejection in Washington, tension also grew between the two opposing groups in the Cherokee Nation. During July of 1835 following a joint meeting at John Ridge's plantation tempers flared and several Treaty supporters were killed. To compound the disruptive circumstances within the Nation, the Georgia legislature passed laws directed at eliminating the Cherokee government and severely restricting the rights of its citizens. Further meetings between the pro and anti removal entities occurred during the summer of 1835 and another with U. S. government officials was scheduled for December. An unusual heavy snowfall prevented most from attending but about 400 men, a significant minority and mostly supporters of the treaty concept, met to discuss possible conditions for removal. On December 29th an agreement was reached deeding Cherokee lands to the government for a financial payment and other stipulations for removal and signed by Treaty Party delegates, among them Major Ridge. Convinced that Andrew Jackson and the United States government would prevail in their efforts to remove Indian tribes, this Cherokee warrior and patriot also knew that land was held in sacred trust by the tribe. He knew firsthand there would be consequences based on the ancient Cherokee Blood Law that decreed death for anyone disposing of public lands without consent of the Nation. Ironically, it was at his request that a statement to that effect be included in the Cherokee Constitution in 1829. Consequently, after affixing his signature to the document Ridge remarked, "I have signed my own death warrant." As events unfolded, his prediction proved to be a self fulfilling prophecy. As Cunningham[4] notes:

> It is significant to observe that it was Major Ridge, one of the staunch defenders of the rights of the Cherokees, who, in 1829, introduced to the National Council meeting at New Echota, a measure decreeing death to any member who would sign a treaty agreeing to give up their country in the East. This measure was adopted.

Fearing for his life and that of his family, in 1837 Ridge migrated from his plantation in Georgia, following the river route to Indian Territory and relocated on Honey Creek in present day Delaware County. There with his son John, he developed a farm and established a trading post that was somewhat isolated from the Cherokee government then located 65 miles south at Park Hill. However, Ridge's movements were not going unnoticed. On June 22, 1839 while riding south on Line Road near today's Dutch Mills, Arkansas, he was assassinated as part of a well organized conspiracy that also took the lives of his son John and Elias Boudinot that same day. Major Ridge, now 68, was buried at Piney Cemetery near New Hope Mission. Several years later his body was exhumed and he was laid to rest near his son John at Polson Cemetery in Delaware County.

Although Major Ridge was of mixed blood and adopted European-American culture, he was first and foremost a proud Cherokee, a fearless warrior, a firm believer in Cherokee traditions and initially an opponent of United States government proposals for removal. From the time he was appointed to the Cherokee National Council in 1792 he developed a popular reputation for advocating Cherokee laws and traditions. However, by 1830 and over a period of ten years, Ridge became convinced that, between continued state and federal governmental pressure and a huge influx of white settlers, the Cherokee needed to negotiate a settlement and move. His decision and stature in the Nation undoubtedly attracted others and over a period of five years the movement grew resulting in a small segment of Cherokee who became known as the "Treaty Party." The decision of Major Ridge and others regarding the Treaty of New Echota resulted in bitter division within the Nation through decades of Cherokee history, and at times still resonates.

John Ross (Kooweskoowe)

Probably the most recognizable Pathfinder of Northeastern Oklahoma is John Ross, who served his people in various capacities for 51 years. The fact that he was mostly of Scotch ancestry, only 1/8 Cherokee, and bore little physical resemblance to his constituents makes their trust in his leadership somewhat more remarkable. Born October 3, 1790, to Daniel Ross and Mollie McDonald John, one of nine children, was raised near present-day Chattanooga, Tennessee. As a young adult, he was given the Cherokee name of Kooweskoowe. Many years later, one of the districts in the young Cherokee Nation would be named Cooweescoowee in his honor. Educated by private tutors and at boarding schools, Ross soon demonstrated an

John Ross

interest in merchandising and developed a partnership with Timothy Meigs, the son of Return Meigs, United States agent to the Cherokees. The two engaged in a lucrative business with the assistance of government contracts. During the Red Stick war of 1814, he participated in the Battle of Horseshoe Bend as a lieutenant in the mounted Cherokees, further burnishing his credentials as a loyal citizen of the Nation. In 1813 Ross married Elizabeth Henley, known better by her nickname, Quatie. The couple had six children but as years passed, they drifted apart, John concentrating on his duties in governmental affairs, Quatie on the family.

In 1815 Ross' first political assignment came at the age of 25 as a member of a Cherokee delegation to the federal government. Committed to their standards and traditions, although his short stature and inability to speak the language were handicaps, he soon became a valued representative of the Cherokee Nation. Conversely, his command of the English language set him apart from other members and enabled him to be a key participant in written negotiations thus launching the first stage of his career in politics. Many years later in 1841, Major Ethan Allen Hitchcock[5], a special government agent sent to the Cherokee Nation to observe and investigate allegations of fraud by Indian agents, reported his impression of John Ross:

> ...is of mixed blood between 45–50 years of age—
> is under size and his manners, unless excited, have
> a dash of diffidence in them—is not of ready speech
> – speaks English principally and will not trust himself
> to address his own people in Cherokee—is a man of
> strong passions and settled purposes which he pursues
> with untiring zeal.

Hitchcock concludes his observations by noting, "After much attentive observation I am of opinion that John Ross is an honest man and a patriot laboring for the good of his people."

As his stock rose among the Cherokee leadership, in addition to legislative duties he was assigned as clerk to Chief Pathkiller and Charles Hicks, and later became president of the National Committee. After the adoption of a new constitution in 1827 the National Committee and the National Council comprised the governing body of the Nation, consequently Ross' became even more politically visible. In January of that year Pathkiller died and Hicks shortly thereafter. Provisions of the new constitution called for an election for chief in 1828. William Hicks, Charles' son and John Ross were nominated and Ross was the overwhelming choice, beginning a career spanning nearly half a century.

With Sequoyah's successful effort to create a Cherokee alphabet several years earlier and the assistance of the *Cherokee Phoenix*, the general public was able to be informed of many issues involving relations between the Nation and the United States government. This medium underscored Ross' many attempts to maintain Cherokee independence on their behalf thus continuing to enhance his popularity.

Ross' stature was not diminished by Cherokee removal to Indian Territory. The disagreement between the Ross faction and their efforts to maintain Cherokee sovereignty to remain in Georgia and Treaty Party advocates seeking conditions for removal have been well documented as have the heinous acts of the United States government prior to removal. Consequently, the fact that John Ross was still able to renegotiate with the federal government after the first stages of actual removal and implement a more viable plan to relocate Cherokee families underscores that he was still recognized as the tribal leader. The Treaty Party members had only been useful to the government in obtaining Cherokee signatures to validate a questionable treaty, which as noted earlier was a proposal that would be ratified by only one vote in the United States Senate.

After the departure of the last of 13 of 1,000 contingents, in December of 1838 under Ross' plan, he followed by riverboat with his family, boxes of national documents, and over 200 tribal members who were too old, sick or lame to travel on foot. Unfortunately, his wife Quatie died of pneumonia and was buried at Little Rock. The remaining passengers arrived in Indian Territory in March of 1839.

Upon the arrival of the Eastern Cherokee, for the next two years disagreements occurred with the Western Cherokee, the "Old Settlers," over by whom and how the government of the Nation would be organized. Of equal concern was the payment for subsidies, land and improvements stipulated in the Treaty of New Echota. In November of 1841, after an extended stay in Washington, Ross and members of the negotiations committee were able to return with both an agreement and confirmation of negotiated funds. But these successes still did not appease many Old Settlers who were still vehemently opposed to the Ross government. During the election of 1843, which Ross won, one of his supporters was killed and another severely beaten in the Saline district while both were serving as election superintendents. Unfortunately ill feelings regarding the Echota treaty were still also a major issue evidenced by the assassination of Thomas Watie, Stand Watie's brother in 1845, that signaled that the "blood law" was still being invoked. In fact, with exception of the Civil War, the violence of Cherokee against Cherokee from 1843 to 1846 was the bloodiest the new Nation experienced. Moulton[6] reports, "Violence finally reached such intensity that the Cherokee agent reported in one ten-month period in 1845-46, a total of thirty four killings occurred, mainly of a political nature." The mayhem continued until finally the Treaty Party sympathizers joined with the Old Settlers and sent a delegation to Washington to propose dividing the Nation. However, through compromise and mutual approval of the Treaty of 1846, the two factions pledged to maintain the Nation as one.

It was within this environment that in 1844, the widower Ross married Mary "Mollie" Stapler, 36 years his junior. The couple resided at Rose Cottage in Park Hill, a large two story home that could accommodate many guests, but they would frequently be separated for months due to Ross' responsibilities representing the Nation in Washington.

The Treaty of 1846 introduced an era of peace that lasted until the Civil War. Ross, as Principal Chief, steered the Nation through negotiations in Washington and through governance issues back home. During these years, both Ross and the Nation began to prosper. In addition to personal business holdings, Ross maintained a large portion of his wealth in slaves and improved land. Under Cherokee law the land belonged to the Nation, but improvements were the property of the individual. This period of peace also resonated with the United States government. Since it appeared that the Cherokee government was developing successfully, in 1857 Fort Gibson was abandoned and the site returned to the Cherokee Nation. But the interlude would be brief because the winds of war were stirring within the United States and the fort, as well as the Nation would soon be embroiled in a civil war.

When war was declared the Cherokee government was pressed by factions within the Nation to join both sides, but Ross favored neutrality. However, eventually he relented and under pressure joined with the other four Civilized Tribes to support the Confederacy. Because of the war, once again lines were drawn between factions within the Nation. The issues were not just about containing slavery or later of freeing the slaves, it also reignited controversy over the Treaty of New Echota. Under pressure from several factions, Ross agreed to join the Confederacy. But by the summer of 1862, the divisiveness and conflicts among various factions within the Nation convinced Ross that his government was in a state of chaos. As a result, Ross defected to the Union, fleeing first to Kansas then Washington until the end of the War. Following the war years and returning to a totally devastated Nation in the fall of 1865 to assist in negotiating peace terms with the Union, the old Chief's advice was virtually ignored. The same situation occurred later that year when he returned to Washington leading still another delegation attempting to negotiate terms of peace. But time had taken its toll on his health. The 75 year old John Ross died August 1, 1866, and was buried near Wilmington, Delaware. His remains were later interred in the Ross Cemetery in Park Hill in 1867.

Ross' tireless efforts to establish the Cherokee Nation as a sovereign entity in the southeastern United States and his later attempts to prevent removal led to his being recognized overwhelmingly by citizens as their leader. His endeavors to negotiate with the government in good faith usually did not succeed because of the vacillating policies and questionable motives of the individuals with whom he dealt. United States officials, pressured by a flood of European immigrants and coveting Indian lands continually broke agreements with tribes or never fulfilled their intent. Like most public officials who serve long terms, Ross was accused of numerous improprieties by his detractors. But elections from 1828 until his death in 1866 still proved him to be the overwhelming choice over his opponents. Throughout his life in government he upheld Cherokee traditions and the majority, particularly the traditionalists, recognized that fact. The quality of his leadership is obvious when reviewing the progress in the development of the new Nation prior to the devastation initiated by the Civil War. He would be pleased with the revitalization of the Cherokee Nation today through evidence of its sovereignty as a nation within a nation and the services now being rendered to its citizens.

Stand Watie (De-ga-ta-ga)

The son of David Uwatie and Susannah Reese, and a nephew of Major Ridge, Stand Watie or Takertawker meaning "he who stands firm," was born December 12, 1806, near the present site of Rome, Georgia. Even as a child, while being educated at the Brainerd Mission School, Watie would have been fully aware of the dispute between the state of Georgia and the Cherokee Nation that later became a defining moment in his life. An early forecast

Stand Watie

of this future Pathfinders bravery emerged when, as a young man and deputy sheriff, he hunted down and killed the murderer of Sheriff Charles Hicks. Later, Watie became influential as clerk of the National Supreme Court and then when he was appointed editor of the *Cherokee Phoenix* he became an advocate for a treaty and removal to Indian Territory. Stand Watie confirmed his position by signing the final version of the Treaty of New Echota during March of 1836. Now, recognizing that living in Georgia would no longer be safe because of the Cherokee National Council's edict of death for anyone unauthorized to sell Cherokee land, he moved to Indian Territory in 1837. By this time Watie had been married twice, his first wife Elizabeth Fields died during childbirth in 1836 and he was separated from the second, Isabella Hicks, when he chose to migrate to Indian Territory. Although Watie was a prominent figure during the dispute over the sale of Cherokee lands, he would even become much more influential and controversial in his new home.

Joining his brother Elias Boudinot who relocated in 1836, Watie aligned himself with the Western Cherokees by opening a store at Park Hill, but a peaceful transition to his new home would soon elude him. Shortly after the forced removal of the tribe and the infamous, Trail of Tears, on June 22, 1839, forewarned by friends Watie, John Bell and George Adair barely escaped a concerted assassination attempt. The same attempt claimed the lives of three other treaty signers, including his brother, Elias Boudinot, Major Ridge and Ridge's son John.

The assassinations proved to be a defining moment between the traditionalists and treaty sympathizers and Watie became identified as the treaty leader for the remainder of his life. Sporadic harassment between the two factions continued and in 1842 Watie was accused of the murder of Jim Foreman, alleged to have been one of Major Ridge's assassins. Fortunately for him the killing occurred in Arkansas and a less biased jury found him not guilty on the basis of self defense. In September, four months after his acquittal, he was married for the third time to

Sarah Bell. The couple would have five children.

Other sporadic murders involving treaty signers or sympathizers followed until finally Watie and Chief John Ross joined in what proved to be an uneasy truce between the two factions. The Cherokee leadership then began to focus on the governance and organization of this new Nation. Laws were passed, an education system developed and the Nation enjoyed a period of relative peace and prosperity. By 1861 the long standing feud over slavery resulted in civil war within the United States and it also enveloped the territory of the Five Tribes. The war created a new division within the Cherokee Nation and although neutrality was briefly discussed the persuasiveness of advocates for the South dominated. Unfortunately, the long standing rancor over the treaty coupled with the issue of slavery resulted in unimaginable acts of cruelty meted out by both factions. This circumstance coupled with skirmishes involving Union troops and the depredations of bushwhackers resulted in total destruction of the infrastructure of the Cherokee Nation.

The Civil War fought in the trans-Mississippi region proved to be Watie's finest hour as a leader. With virtually no assistance from the Confederacy, he led Confederate troops in unprecedented guerrilla warfare tactics for the next four years earning the rank of brigadier general. Later, engaging in peace time negotiations during the fall of 1865 and although he had led the confederate cause, Watie and his nephew Elias C. Boudinot obtained favorable peace terms from the federal government.

The post war and Watie's declining years proved to be unkind, a series of setbacks in farming and a failed attempt to establish a tobacco factory with Boudinot plagued the general as he fought to rebuild his life. Compounding his misfortunes, all three of his sons died before Watie's own death in 1871.

From the time he served as deputy sheriff and occupied other important offices in the Eastern Cherokee Nation it was obvious that Stand Watie, "he who stands firm," would be a recognized leader throughout his life. After relocating to Indian Territory, the mantle of leadership of the "Treaty Party" was again pressed upon him following the assassinations of June, 1839. Subsequently, the Civil War thrust him into even more responsibility and his tactics in warfare led to successes that ultimately earned him the promotion to Confederate brigadier general. His capture of a million dollar wagon train during the Second Battle of Cabin Creek in 1864 with the able assistance of Richard Gano earned many plaudits from Confederate officials. Cunningham[4] notes:

> General E. Kirby-Smith termed the capture of the wagon train one of the most brilliant raids of the war,' adding, The celebrity of the movement, the dash of the attack and their entire success entitle the commands engaged to the thanks of the country.

Thrust into leadership responsibilities from his youth to advanced age, Stand Watie, through both decisions and actions, contributed enormously to the young Cherokee Nation.

Sequoyah

Perhaps the most nationally well known of any of the leadership among the Cherokee Tribe, there appears to be as many theories about the early life of Sequoyah as there are biographers who write about him. But all agree that as a young man he developed the Cherokee syllabary. Thought to have been born around 1770 in Tuskegee near the British Fort Loudoun as George Guess or Gist, eventually he signed his name *Siquoya*, from the Cherokee word, *siqua* meaning "hog." There are various versions regarding the background of his parents. One is that his father was an itinerant German peddler named Nathaniel Gist who was absent when Sequoyah was born. His mother's name was Wut-the and Sequoyah was the only child born to the couple. Some biographers indicate that Sequoyah as a young man married Sally Benge and the couple had four children, a second marriage to U-ti-yu produced three more.

Sequoyah

During the early years of his life his mother ran a trading post. As Sequoyah grew to manhood it became apparent that he was a talented craftsman, he learned how to make jewelry and was a noted silversmith. Following his mother's death Sequoyah took over the trading post but he also acquired a bad drinking habit that he eventually overcame. He also participated with the Cherokee regiment participating in the Battle of Horseshoe Bend during the Creek War of 1813-14.

Sequoyah first became interested in the written word while dealing with white settlers and traders, referring to the printed materials they had as "talking leaves." In 1809 he began his first attempt to develop a way for Cherokees to also talk on paper. His early efforts failed when he tried to convert entire written words into Cherokee, later he succeeded when he listed 86 characters instead, one for each syllable.

Unable to convince fellow tribesman in Georgia to even attempt to learn the syllabary, he and his six year old daughter who had learned it, traveled to Arkansas where the Western Cherokee were living to try and convince the leadership of the practicality of his findings. As before, the tribesman did not take him seriously until, after writing down words they gave him, he called his daughter into the room and she read them, convincing those present.

Returning to the Eastern Cherokee in the early 1820s, he then convinced the leadership of the usefulness of the system and soon thereafter copies of the laws of the Cherokee Nation were developed using the syllabary. Until it was developed, only those with the ability to read English were capable of understanding the written word. However, a newspaper, the *Cherokee Phoenix,* initiated publication and was circulated throughout the Nation thus enabling those who learned the syllabary to read about contemporary events. The publication proved to be timely in light of all of the events that occurred prior to the Nation's removal to Indian Territory.

A firm believer in Cherokee traditions, in 1825 Sequoyah

moved to Arkansas to live with the Western Cherokee. When they relocated to Indian Territory in 1828 he built a cabin near today's Sallisaw. In addition to farming he operated a salt refining business. After the Eastern Cherokee moved, Sequoyah and Reverend Jesse Bushyhead were instrumental in convincing both Eastern and Western Cherokee to resolve their differences regarding governing the new Nation at a tribal meeting during the summer of 1839.

It had long been a dream of Sequoyah's to reunite factions of the Cherokee Tribe who fled during various attempts by the federal government to remove tribes to the west. One group fled to Texas then Mexico so he and several companions journeyed to Mexico in an attempt to persuade them to return to the new Cherokee Nation. Leaving Park Hill in April, 1842, they traveled west to the vicinity of present day Oklahoma City then southwest to Mexico. During the journey Sequoyah, now thought to be 73 years old, became increasingly ill and, soon after arriving in Zaragosa, Mexico he died and was buried there.

Sequoyah's gift of a "talking leaves" was a major contribution toward unifying his people. While mission educated Cherokee became literate in English, the majority, those who did not attend school, remained illiterate. This division created difficulties in communication that often led to misunderstandings about contemporary events and decisions that resulted. Therefore communication was vastly improved with his syllabary. It proved to be easy to learn and spread rapidly through the Nation. His contribution prior to the eventual transitioning to Indian Territory enabled citizens to become more informed about events before removal actually began.

A less well known fact was his passion for a united Cherokee Nation. Sequoyah opposed assimilation into the white culture, represented by mixed bloods and that was the primary reason he left Georgia to join Western Cherokees in Arkansas who followed traditional ways. Disturbed by the arguments between Eastern and Western Cherokee after the Trail of Tears, he along with Reverend Jesse Bushyhead was instrumental in initiating the reunification of the two factions. Still concerned about other smaller groups that fled during the previous years of upheaval, he was still attempting to restore unity to the tribe when he died.

BIOGRAPHY

[1]Excerpt from *The Missionary Herald,* containing the Proceedings At Large of the American Board of Commissioners for Foreign Missions; with a General View of Other Benevolent Operations For the Year 1830. Crocker & Brewster. Boston. 1830.

[2]Foreman, Grant. *Pioneer Days in the Early Southwest.* University of Nebraska Press. Lincoln and London. 1994. P. 29 & 30.

[3]Gregory, Jack and Strickland, Rennard. *Sam Houston with the Cherokees, 1829 – 1833.* University of Oklahoma Press. Norman and London. 1995. P. 13.

[4]Cunningham, Frank. *General Stand Watie's Confederate Indians.* University of Oklahoma Press. Norman. 1998. P. 15. P. 159.

[5]Hitchcock, Ethan Allen, edited by Grant Foreman. *A Traveler in Indian Territory, the Journal of Ethan Allen Hitchcock.* University of Oklahoma Press. Norman and London. 1996. P. 234.

[6]Moulton, Gary E. *John Ross, Cherokee Chief.* Brown Thrasher Books. The University of Georgia Press. 1978. p. 149.

CHAPTER 5

God's Emissaries

"And he said unto them, go ye into all the world and preach the gospel to every creature."

Gospel of Mark, Chapter 16, Verse 15

Missionary is a term most commonly used to define the work of those sent into an area to perform services such as religious education or social services by Christian missions. In one form or another, these advocates, have been active since shortly after the crucifixion of Jesus and the transformation of Paul. First, known as disciples, later as apostles, they sought to convert those who would listen to their version of what soon became known as Christianity. Their contact with possible converts was verbal, stories handed down over time coupled with their personal interpretations of Jesus' teachings.

Biblical historians generally agree that it was at least 55 to 65 years after his death before the first written account of Jesus' life, the Gospel of Mark, was written. Mark, thought to be a traveling companion of Paul wrote his gospel in Greek, the universal language at that time. It was nearly 400 years after his death before a combination of two books, four gospels and 21 epistles or letters, 13 ascribed to the apostle Paul, were finally combined into a canon called the New Testament. And for over 1,000 years afterward individual copies of both the Old and New Testaments were laboriously developed in long hand, leaving to the imagination whether or not each copy was accurately reproduced. It wasn't until Guttenberg invented the printing press and printed his first bible in 1454 that a standard printed version could readily be made in exact duplicate for the benefit of those who were literate. From that time forward, missionaries, including those eventually assigned to the Cherokee, could go forth preaching their interpretation of Christianity but with a unified reference.

History is rife with the deeds and misdeeds of Christian missionaries conducted on behalf of their beliefs. Some provided exemplary service to converts, some were martyred and others sought to use force to "convert" the unbeliever. The Baltic Crusades, Spanish Inquisition, and invasion of several South American countries bear evidence of the heinous acts committed by those zealots.

There are numerous interpretations that fall under the umbrella of Christianity but the common thread is a belief in a supreme being and an afterlife. Belief in a supreme being was not reserved just for European Christians. Aboriginal tribes worldwide also worshipped their concept of a creator or higher being. But like the Romans who worshipped a myriad of gods, prior to the introduction of Christianity, there were also Native American tribes, fearing a variety of vengeful spirits, who held pagan rituals and recognized many gods.

In America a small group of Moravian missionaries arrived in the region inhabited by the Cherokee in 1735 and lived in Savannah for a decade before leaving. They returned in 1800 and founded the first mission in the Cherokee Nation at Spring Place in Georgia. From the time of their arrival the Moravians found religious compatibility with the Cherokee in some aspects. Missionaries discovered tribal members prayed to one God of creation and believed in an afterlife. According to Nakai Breen, a famous Cherokee elder[1], "The devotion of the Cherokee people was to the Supreme Holy Spirit who could not be looked upon and whose energy was the fire of all creation and the fire of all life and who reside in the heavens and on earth through purified people." The background of their beliefs also somewhat paralleled those found in the history of the Old Testament. They had a version of the first humans on earth comparable to Adam and Eve although the female was neither constructed from the male (Adam's rib) nor subservient to him. The Cherokee believed Kana'ti, the first man, provided game and Selu, the first women, provided corn and beans. Both contributed equally according to the Cherokee origins.

The second missionary site in the Cherokee Nation, Brainerd Mission, was founded near present day Chattanooga, Tennessee in 1817 by Reverend Cyrus Kingsbury, representing the American Board of Commissioners for Foreign Missions (ABCFM). The mission combined the teaching of Christianity with general education, a popular combination particularly with mixed blood tribesman. Other missionaries followed and as they became more familiar with the Cherokee and knowledgeable about repressive measures taken against the tribe by the federal government and the state of Georgia, they also became strong advocates for Cherokee sovereignty. In fact, prior to passage of the Indian Removal Act of 1830 the ABCFM led an extensive battle in congress lobbying against removal. Their efforts nearly succeeded when the Act only passed by one vote in the United States senate. And, in 1831 several missionaries were imprisoned in Georgia for violating one of several insidious laws, this one forbidding whites from entering and living in Cherokee Territory without a Georgia state license. Recognizing the sovereignty of the Cherokee Nation that had previously been accepted by the United States, the Georgia law was overturned by the Supreme Court but that ruling was conveniently ignored by both President Jackson and the State of Georgia.

When it became evident to some tribesmen that the oppression would not cease, they moved west into Arkansas Territory and several missionaries accompanied them. Later, as witnesses to what would forever be a stain on American moral integrity, other missionaries watched helplessly as both white citizens and soldiers, armed with legislated and military authority ransacked homes, stole property and imprisoned Cherokees in open air stockades before they were eventually deported west. Some missionaries were also incarcerated with them until the Cherokee were released to begin the long journey. While a few remained behind to minister to some, most true to their own principles of service either led or accompanied contingents bound for Indian Territory. Some documented the horrors of the journey that later became known as the "Trail of Tears." Their observations of what happened both before and after provided objective evidence of the inhumane conditions foisted on the Cherokee and many other displaced tribes by the United States government. This was an act of force and retribution not so far removed from the Nazi Kristallnacht (night of the broken glass) forced on German Jews by the Nazi's a century later.

Perhaps the greatest contribution missionaries made to the Cherokee Nation followed the removal of the tribe to Indian Territory. They built missions and not only became trusted religious leaders and educators but some became involved politically. They became credible eye witnesses to the unfulfilled promises of the government and the chicanery of federal agents assigned to implement them. They used their talents to continue to educate and to teach their versions of Christianity by using the printed word initiated by Sequoyah's alphabet. They assisted in initiating a democratic form of government and developing a formal education system. And they administered to both the relocated Cherokee and indigenous Osage tribes. Although the biographies of only a select few are reflected on the following pages, the lasting memorial for those mentioned and their colleagues resonate not only through their names and deeds but places they founded in the new Nation such as Dwight, Fairfield, Hopefield and Union missions.

Daniel Butrick

Daniel Butrick was born in Massachusetts in 1789 and educated at the Cooperstown Academy in New York. Ordained in 1817, he arrived at the recently constructed Brainerd Mission in Tennessee during January of 1818. In addition to Brainerd, he later served at several other Cherokee Nation mission stations. On April 27, 1827, he was married to Elizabeth Proctor, mission teacher. In their respective capacities as minister and teacher, the Butricks served the Cherokees in Georgia for a combined 35 years, Daniel for twenty and Elizabeth for fifteen. Even though many of the ABCFM missionaries left for Indian Territory in 1836 following the signing of the Treaty of New Echota, Butrick and his wife, both staunchly in favor of the traditionalist position against the Echota treaty, elected to remain with their congregation.

During the transition period in 1838 General Winfield Scott was placed in charge of the Cherokee removal. According to Foreman[2]:

> His orders were intended to quickly end the drawn out process of removal and it provided at least one element under his command, the Georgia Militia, the opportunity to immediately enforce brutal tactics. Under the scrutiny of the militia families were driven from their homes without warning, marched to open air stockades and imprisoned with the clothes on their backs and whatever they could carry. Meanwhile, Georgia citizens were stealing anything of worth and driving off livestock for themselves. The result was absolute chaos. Fortunately, after three contingents of tribesmen were removed during the summer of 1838

with disastrous results, Chief John Ross was able to negotiate an alternative solution for removal of the majority.

Although the contributions of the Butricks during their years in Georgia were significant, a journal of the events prior to and during removal has proven to be even more so. Through his written observations, Daniel Butrick has provided an eyewitness written account of arguably the most egregious event in American history. Even before his journey, as a staunch supporter of the traditionalist viewpoint he led his church members in passing a resolution that they would not associate with treaty signers unless they recanted. He comments further about that issue in his journal. But first and foremost, he captures the horrific acts of United States soldiers and Georgia militia as they force families from their homes without forewarning and imprison them in stockades. Deciding to join his parishioners in their westward venture, Butrick recounts the journey of one contingent of Cherokees led by Richard Taylor that he and Elizabeth accompanied to Indian Territory. The Trail of Tears Association[3] has reprinted his observations, 83 written before Taylor's detachment left and 127 during the journey.

Following are some of the excerpts that describe the imprisonment of Cherokees and events prior to departure:

> May 26, 1838, p. 1
> Brainerd Mission
>
> ...As the soldiers advanced toward a house, two little children fled in fright to the woods. The women pleaded for permission to seek them, or wait until they came in, giving positive assurances that she would then follow on, and join the company. But all entreaties were in vain; and it was not until a day or two after that she would get permission for one of her friends to go back after the lost children.
>
> ...A man deaf and dumb, being surprised at the approach of armed men, attempted to make his escape,

and because he did not hear and obey the command of his pursuers, was shot dead on the spot.

...Cattle, horses, hogs, household furniture clothing and money not with them when taken were left. And it is said that the white inhabitants around, stood with open arms to seize whatever property they could put their hands on.

...Those taken to the fort at New Echota, were confined day and night in the open air, with but little clothing to cover them, when lying on the naked ground.

Reverend Butrick continues to describe the wanton destruction, mistreatment, rape and death during the summer months, as he observed similar atrocities. He relates multiple instances of complete indifference to the needs of many young and elderly who are allowed to die for lack of medical assistance:

Monday, September 3, p. 34

Unbelievable Conditions

...Dear little infants; O how distressing to see their feeble little hands holding to their mothers bosoms, and pulling back to life, while ruthless monsters snatched them away and drove them lonely to the grave. Thus, when the dear little ones were sick in the last company driven from the landing, they were taken it is said, from the mother's arms and thrown into wagons and driven over rough roads there, in that torturing wagon, the suffering infant must lie and die, unnurtured, and at night be take out and put away in a lonely tomb.

Earlier, the first of three detachments coordinated under General Scott, numbering about 800, journeyed by river and were supervised by government troops. They boarded boats on June 6, 1838, and after a perilous journey, that accounted for many deaths, arrived at Fort Smith on the 19th. The second detachment left on June 13, but encountered even more delays and didn't arrive until August 5. The third detachment was confronted with so many more logistical problems prior to its arrival in Indian Territory that it was then that Cherokee leadership successfully negotiated with General Scott who agreed to let them supervise their own removal.

As a result 13 detachments numbering approximately 1,000 each were organized under the supervision of John Ross and other Cherokee officials. Daniel and Elizabeth obtained approval to travel with Taylor's contingent that departed October 11, 1838. They would travel the northernmost route first to Nashville, Tennessee, across Kentucky and Illinois, crossing the Mississippi River, then northwest through Rolla and Springfield, Missouri, and on to Arkansas.

Although all detachments were typically subjected to price gouging by merchants along the way, after nearly a month traveling west Butrick describes what proved to be an occasional instance of charity near Nashville:

> Wednesday, November 21, p. 46
>
> Nashville, Tennessee
>
> ...Mrs. Bryant and the other ladies had brought clothing to give to the needy Cherokees though they said they found none needy in this detachment, compared with other companies that had gone on."

But much more frequently the detachment met not only with unreasonable prices but harassment as Butrick continues to explain:

> Saturday, December 15, p. 49
>
> Crossing the Ohio River
>
> ...Those of us who crossed first went on to the place designated for camping about a mile & a half from the river. I immediately commenced gathering wood for the Sabbath. Having done this, & commenced making preparation for supper, we were told by a white man living near, that was not the place for camping, but we must go beyond the next plantation.

The same circumstance occurred again when they reached the next site that afternoon, only to be told to move on a third time to public land. Inhospitality was also occasionally accompanied by murder. In isolated instances local residents would kill older Cherokees in camp claiming they died from natural causes, then demand a fee for burying them.

Finally, on January 26, 1839, after a journey lasting 113 days the Taylor detachment crossed the Mississippi River near Cape Girardeau, Missouri. Traveling northwest through the month of February, they arrived at Springfield, Missouri, which Butrick described as "a pleasant village," then turned southwest reaching the border of Indian Territory near today's Westville on March 30:

> Monday, April 1 p. 64
> Westville, I.T.
> ...We made arrangements to send Jonas, the little boy who came with us, to his father; gave our tent to an old Cherokee woman, who had none, & took our leave of the dear detachment with whom we had been wondering these last months.

Throughout their professional lives, Daniel and Elizabeth Butrick remained dedicated to converting and educating the Cherokee people. When animosities between the United States government and the Cherokee Nation concluded in the violent acts that led to removal, their allegiance was clearly with their chosen constituents and their stewardship was unflagging. However, of equal importance is Daniel's detailed and objective journal chronicling an important historic event. Daniel and Elizabeth Butrick continued to serve their chosen constituents for many years, first at Fairfield Mission in today's Adair County and later at Beattie's Prairie in Delaware County. Elizabeth died in 1847 and Daniel in 1851. Both are buried at the Dwight Mission cemetery in Sequoyah County.

Cephas Washburn

Cephas Washburn was one of the first missionaries to assist the Cherokee west of the Mississippi River. Born July 25, 1793 in Vermont, he was ordained in 1818 and married Abigail Woodward in October of that year. First cousins, the couple were descendants of forbearers who arrived in America aboard the Mayflower in 1620. Immediately after the marriage the Washburn's were sent by the ABCFM to minister to the Cherokees at Brainerd Mission in Georgia. That same year Tahlonteskee, the Principal Chief of the Western Cherokee visited Brainerd and requested that a mission be constructed in western Arkansas Territory. Many tribesmen or "Western Cherokee" had been moving to the region for years and a recently negotiated treaty with the United States called for their removal even further west in Arkansas Territory. The assignment fell to Cephas and Abigail and during the summer of 1819, traveling by steamer and keel boat, they arrived at a site near today's Clarksville. Thus began the history of the Dwight Mission, eventually moved and still currently remaining in what soon would be designated as the Cherokee Nation.

The Washburn's were greeted by a less than enthusiastic Cherokee War Chief, Takatoka. Chief Tahlonteskee, who requested the mission, died during the spring of 1819. The War Chief and some of his cohorts had misgivings that a mission, focusing on education and Christianity, might divert children from a clear understanding of their Cherokee heritage. However, John Jolly, Tahlonteskee's brother, recently elected as tribal Civil Chief of Internal Affairs and Diplomacy, was very supportive. Eventually the war chief's concerns were satisfied and construction of the mission proceeded.

The site of the mission, chosen in 1820 by Washburn and his associate Alfred Finney was named for Timothy Dwight, former president of Yale University and the first corporate member of ABCFM. When it was completed in 1824 there were at least 24 buildings in the small town that included every necessary facility from a church to blacksmith shop. The school offered classes in reading, arithmetic, farming skills, carpentry, blacksmithing, sewing and cooking. During its brief existence in Arkansas Territory the school enrollment ranged from 20 to 100 children.

After negotiations related to the Louisiana Purchase were consummated in 1803, white settlers began rapidly moving west across the Mississippi River into new territories that it bordered, including Arkansas. To accommodate this surge, in 1828 still another treaty was negotiated between the government and the Western Cherokee that moved them further west to the region set aside and designated for the tribe in Indian Territory. The original Dwight Mission in Arkansas was closed in 1829 and, under Washburn's supervision, was relocated on Sallisaw Creek near present day Sallisaw, Oklahoma. The school reopened during the spring of 1830 and the mission eventually included 21 houses and a number of outbuildings that served both the religious and educational needs of the tribe.

Cephas and Abigail Washburn continued to minister and to educate Cherokee children and bore witness to the many horrific events that later involved Cherokee removal. During the summer of 1838, before the Cherokee leadership negotiated an alternate plan with General Scott, the second of three parties coordinated by the U.S. Army arrived near Dwight Mission in late July. Mute evidence of those statistics reflect to what degree the "heavy handed" tactics of the army's removal methods succeeded. Eight hundred seventy five tribesmen began the journey in Georgia but only 602 arrived in Indian Territory. Foreman[2], quoting from Cephas Washburn's journal regarding the event noted:

> Just returned from a neighborhood about ten miles from the mission where there have been fourteen deaths within three weeks…want of medical aid… since last October about 2,000 immigrants have come. Twenty-five hundred more are on their way…much

Cephas Washburn
Superintendent, Dwight Mission

sickness and mortality among them.

The Washburns and others at the mission provided as much relief as their resources would permit.

During the early stages of the Civil War, many of the mission buildings were destroyed and the mission was closed. In 1884, it was reopened and new buildings, including a boarding school, were constructed. It remained open as a training school for Indian students until 1948. Today, Dwight Mission is operated as a Presbyterian camp and conference center.

Although Cephas Washburn is most closely identified with the founding of the mission, he also actively pursued another education endeavor called the Far West Seminary. By 1843, he joined prominent citizens in the state of Arkansas in an attempt to create a school of higher education. The school was envisioned to include classical education, as well as instruction in agriculture and the mechanical arts. Although it received a state charter and despite a financial depression, to compound matters, while the ill fated project was under construction, a fire destroyed the nearly completed structure. Further efforts to rebuild it were abandoned.

The Reverend Cephas and Abigail Washburn clearly typify an example of "God's Emissaries," as evidenced by their complete dedication to improving the religious and educational status of the Cherokee regardless of where they were sent. The two worked tirelessly constructing the Dwight Mission first in Arkansas, then reconstructing it in Indian Territory where it still remains as a religious and educational center. Cephas also continued his efforts to promote education through an attempt to found the first center of higher education. Although it failed to materialize, the project provided the precedent for other educational institutions in Fayetteville, that later earned the community the title, "the Athens of Arkansas."

From 1850 to 1856, Cephas Washburn served as minister of the First Presbyterian Church in Fort Smith, Arkansas. He died in 1860 and is buried at Little Rock. Abigail Woodward

Washburn succeeded him in her missionary endeavors for another 19 years until 1879 and is buried in the Washburn Cemetery near Russellville.

Epaphras Chapman

Epaphras Chapman was born during April of 1792 and lived in East Haddam, Connecticut. In 1819 the United Foreign Missionary Society, later absorbed by ABCFM, sent the 27 year old Chapman and Job Vinall, to locate a mission site in Indian Territory that would be suitable to administer to the Osage Tribe. Vinall fell ill and died of fever at Fort Smith during the journey. However, with the assistance of Nathaniel Pryor, Chapman continued to search for a location and they selected a site on the Grand River near Mission Bend about 25 miles north of Three Forks that he named Union Mission. As time would prove, the site that was chosen would be not only unhealthy but controversial as a site to administer to the Osage. As if a precursor of things to come, Chapman, the founder and leader of Union Mission would die in 1826 at the age of 32. Like several others who served at Union Mission, Chapman became a victim of what was then diagnosed as "intermittent fever," later determined to be malaria carried by the ever present crop of mosquitoes at the site.

The controversy related to the success of the mission concerns an agreement that William Lovely, the sub-agent for the Cherokee had taken upon himself to develop before Union Mission was even founded. For centuries the Osage had claimed Arkansas Territory as a portion of their vast Nation and frequently battled the Quapaw over it. In addition, at the turn of the 19th century a substantial number of Osage tribesmen, encouraged by Jean Chouteau and led by Chiefs Clermont and Cashesegra, moved from western Missouri to locations in the vicinity of the Verdigris River to hunt and trap. Consequently, when the Western

Cherokee moved to western Arkansas in the same general proximity, there were frequent clashes between the two tribes. In 1816, in order to attempt a resolution, Lovely negotiated an agreement between the warring factions whereby the Osage would deed seven million acres of land to the Cherokee to settle past depredations. The area, known as Lovely's Purchase, and eventually approved by Congress in 1824, covered a region from the Verdigris River to Arkansas Territory that included the site of the future Union Mission. So it became problematic that Union Mission, built to serve the Osage was actually on disputed land supposedly ceded to their enemies, the Cherokee. Technicalities aside, the Cherokee devised their own solution to the problem. During October of 1817, because the Osage continued to attack Cherokee villages and farms thus disregarding the agreement, the Cherokee and a coalition of other tribes, totaling a force of over 600, attacked and decimated the village of Osage war chief Clermont. Both Lovely's arrangement and the Cherokee attack preceded Chapman's decision to locate Union Mission at its chosen site in 1819, setting the stage for further conflicts.

After selecting the site, Chapman returned to the East and organized a party of 21 that included his wife, Hannah, carpenters, stone masons, teachers and others who could contribute to the educational and religious objectives of the mission. Leaving the Boston area during the spring of 1820 and traveling by river, the missionary party reached Little Rock in November and the men proceeded to the Grand River site to construct housing. The remainder of the party arrived the following February of 1821. During the winter months the site appeared to be satisfactory with an open meadow, a flowing spring and a salt well, but the following spring would prove there were several drawbacks. The lowland that was chosen adjacent to the river was a haven for mosquitoes and the result was constant sickness among the inhabitants. The timber used originally to construct cabins decayed and eventually it became necessary to float hard wood logs for construction from the Spavinaw area 25 miles upstream.

The inhabitants persisted in their endeavors but conditions at the mission location were still troubling. Holway[4] notes that the Reverend William F. Vaill, the school superintendent reported to the Missionary Society six years after the mission was founded that, "The dwelling houses are about a dozen log cabins, decayed and uncomfortable." He also lists:

> 40' by 60' barn, a well covered frame building
> 12' square spring house, the spring flowing through it
> 20' square storehouse, two story, well covered
> 13' square frame shoemakers shop
> log schoolhouse in poor condition
> kitchen and dining-hall under one roof, built of logs and in a state of decay
> old storehouse, carpenter shop, blacksmith shop, and smokehouse, all of log construction.

Unfortunately, Vaill's somewhat negative assessment of the mission structures would be trumped further by Mother Nature during September of that same year. The worst flood man ever encountered on the Grand River to that time inundated the compound washing away some structures, drowning several domestic animals and ruining most of the necessities for survival.

As if poor location, inferior buildings and Mother Nature weren't barriers enough, the Union missionaries faced other obstacles in their efforts to convert the Osage to becoming self sustaining Christian farmers. Traditionally, Osage warriors, muscular and often nearly seven foot tall, hunted and fought and the women cooked and cultivated. Despite the efforts of the missionaries Osage men were not persuaded that agriculture was in their future. The warriors collective opinion on becoming "tillers of the soil" can be summed up in an incident related in Washington Irving's Journal edited by McDermott[5]. After visiting Union Mission in 1832, Irving writes, "Old Father Vaill preaching to the Indians on the necessity of industry as a means to happiness. One old Indian responded that plowing the fields and building fences was not his idea of happiness."

With limited success but still intent on reforming the Osage, the missionaries constructed a satellite mission in 1823 they named Hopefield that would focus only on teaching farming skills. Established about five miles upstream from Union, there was neither a school nor church at this location. Eleven Osage families relocated there, labored through the summer and were pleasantly surprised at the bountiful harvest they collected in the fall. But the men were constantly harassed by Osage warriors as "field makers" doing the work of women. On occasion, there were ominous threats from other Osage that caused the families to flee to Union Mission for safety. But Hopefield, like Union, also suffered severely during the flood of 1826, so much so that the little settlement was moved further north near the mouth of Cabin Creek, on Grand River but the venture never repeated even its limited earlier success.

To add to the negativism created by fellow tribesmen, white fur traders were also unsupportive because they wanted the Osage men to hunt in order to supply their lucrative fur trade. During his visit Irving noted, "Colonel A. P. Chouteau is said to have remarked disdainfully about two half breeds, that this one had been twice as long at the Mission as the other and therefore is twice as good for nothing."

As if the attitude of the Osage, Mother Nature's vagaries, and previous government negotiations weren't problems enough, there was also growing dissension among the mission occupants themselves regarding their primary objectives. Some believed that schooling and the pursuit of agriculture should be the focus although neither venture ultimately proved very successful. School attendance was sporadic, Holway reports, "Originally intended as the instrument of education for Osage children only, the school was never able to enroll as new pupils more than seventeen Osage children in one year (1826) and during the twelve years of its life only seventy-nine Osage children attended the school, some of these for only a few weeks."

Abraham Redfield, a carpenter by trade and lay preacher, believed the emphasis should be on conversion to Christianity, particularly the Presbyterian version. Dr. Marcus Palmer, the mission doctor, also expressed a desire to go into Indian country to preach the gospel. The Missionary Society back east was inclined to agree, but no changes were made and neither man ventured forth to exercise their bias.

In terms of impact and its longevity, the Union Mission proved to be only marginally successful. Before its founding, the failure of tribal reconciliation through the efforts of William Lovely as well as the indecisiveness of the UMCF leadership regarding the focus of Union Mission became a constant issue with the missionaries on site. The location proved to be a serious problem as the swamp-like conditions resulted in "intermittent fever" that took the lives of many of the mission occupants. The uncooperative attitude of the Osage toward either assimilation into white culture or conversion to Christianity proved to be a constant issue and the lack of support for the assimilation of the Osage by white fur traders was particularly a problem.

Aside from efforts involving the Osage there were some positive aspects. Until the mission was abandoned in 1837, the growing numbers of southbound travelers on the Texas Road utilized it as a camp site to replenish food supplies and to take advantage of medical services. In 1835, the mission served as the location for a printing press operated by Samuel Worcester, the first in the Cherokee Nation. And, although school attendance and efforts at promoting agriculture were disappointing, perhaps after the Osage were relocated to Kansas in 1839, the lessons some learned at Union Mission may have proven useful as they began to assimilate into white culture. Perhaps if he had lived, Epaphras Chapman may have been the catalyst for the positive leadership necessary to assure Union Mission's adjustment to the conditions that existed and to its survival. Today his gravestone in the small cemetery is a mute reminder of that possibility.

Evan Jones

Evan Jones, a Welchman by birth, must be recognized as one of the most influential missionaries, particularly with the full blood Cherokees after his arrival in Indian Territory. He followed a circuitous route to the Cherokee Nation in Georgia. Born in Brecknockshire, Wales in 1788, Jones moved to London to pursue his trade as a haberdasher. There he met and married Elizabeth Lanigan. In 1821, he and his family, now including four children, migrated to the United States and settled in Philadelphia. Shortly after their arrival Jones and his wife relinquished their membership in the Methodist Church and became Baptists. That same year he accepted a position as a teacher for the Baptist Foreign Missionary Board and was assigned to Valley Town, North Carolina. Arriving in September, Jones immediately began to learn the Cherokee language, both speaking the native tongue and memorizing the syllabary that Sequoyah had just completed. This accomplishment would place him in high regard among the Cherokee. Shortly after his arrival, the Baptist Board promoted him to superintendent of the school and later he was ordained as a Baptist minister.

Following John Ross' election as Principal Chief in 1828 and because of his support of Cherokee tradition, Jones became a strong supporter of Ross and his policies. Throughout the 18 years he was involved with the Cherokee, prior to removal, Jones, like many other missionaries, observed the results of the divisive activities and chicanery promoted by both the federal government and the state of Georgia. Jones also was strongly opposed to the Treaty of New Echota, partly due to the terms, but mainly because of the lack of consensus among the majority of the tribe. This further solidified his stature among traditionalists.

Although vigorously supporting the right for the Cherokee to remain in their native land, after all avenues of diplomacy and appeal failed, he volunteered to assist Situwakee in leading one of the Cherokee detachments on the infamous Trail of Tears.

Departing with 1,250 tribesmen from the valley towns of East Tennessee on October 9, 1938, traveling with 62 wagons and 560 horses, 1,033 had survived when the journey ended on February 2, 1839.

He acquired considerable stature before leaving Georgia and the Welchman became even more influential upon reaching Indian Territory. Shortly after the arrival of a contingent led by Reverend Jesse Bushyhead later in February, the two ministers began construction of Baptist Mission. The mission, located a few miles north of present day Westville, near the Arkansas border, soon became known as Ga-du-y ga du or "Breadtown" by the Cherokee because it also became a distribution site for government food rations.

As it evolved, the Baptist Mission also became a center for community activities that included a school, trading post and post office. In order to reach more of his constituents, Jones also developed a circuit of four "preaching stations." Just as before, his fervent Christian teachings and support of Cherokee traditions, as well as a close relationship with Chief John Ross, resonated with full bloods among the tribe.

Jones also organized several schools in the region that focused on teaching and utilizing the Cherokee language. In 1843 he succeeded in obtaining a Cherokee printing press and for a short time, until budget issues forced him to close, Jones initiated a periodical, the *Cherokee Messenger*, that translated school books, a hymnal and religious tracts into the native language. Many of Jones' efforts and interests focused on adults, including organizing several temperance societies to address the problems of alcohol use.

While the Cherokee were primarily occupied with aspects of developing their new Nation, national politics became focused more and more on the issue of slavery. In 1845, it caused division within the Baptist church and the formation of the Southern Baptist Convention whose congregations supported it. Evan Jones was fervently opposed to slavery and prepared fiery

Baptist Mission Church
Indian Territory

sermons against its evils. He became recognized as an outspoken abolitionist who believed that owning slaves conflicted with the teachings of Christ. His influence among a significant number of non-slave holding Cherokee soon made Jones a target of concern for pro-slavery advocates. Their dislike became even more intense when, in 1856, he helped to reinstitute the Keetoowah Society, an organization devoted to maintaining Cherokee traditions that had functioned in the Nation during the years before removal. The Society also declared opposition to slavery. Members of the Keetoowah were identified by crossed pins under the lapels of their coats and soon became known as "pin Indians." Pro-slavery advocates countered by forming a chapter of the Knights of the Golden Circle, an Ohio based group advocating the expansion of slavery, not only into new states but throughout many Caribbean countries. As tensions escalated, and the war approached, the friction reached a climax when a plot was discovered to assassinate Jones and burn Baptist Mission. His close alignment with John Ross and with the Pins convinced him to flee Indian Territory and move to Kansas for safety with his family in 1862.

After the Cherokee Nation aligned with the Confederacy, that same year Chief Ross was also forced to leave the Nation and also move to Kansas. Later, Jones left Kansas with his family, joined Ross in Philadelphia and together, during the war, they sought meetings with government officials, lobbying to secure charitable donations and clothing for Cherokee loyalists. After the war concluded in 1865, he returned to the Nation living in Tahlequah and resuming his ministry. In 1872, fifty one years after dedicating his life to his chosen people, Evan Jones died at the age of 84 and was buried in the local cemetery.

Just as so many of his fellow missionaries, Evan Jones became a tireless advocate for the Cherokee people not only promoting the Christian religion, but also becoming intensely involved in political issues. Unlike many Indian tribes, segments of the Cherokee had initiated assimilation into European culture for at least a century before the organized missionary effort of the early 1800s. Missionaries saw for themselves that many had adapted to the white man's culture, and many were more Caucasian than Indian by birth. Consequently, men like Evan Jones stood firmly against both the rationale and subversive tactics that the United States and Georgia governments were attempting to use to remove the tribe.

Eventually, the failed attempt at retaining the Nation in the southeast led most of the missionaries to join their constituents, many plodding along the Trail of Tears, then carving out a new government in the Cherokee's designated portion of Indian Territory. Upon his arrival, Evan Jones distinguished himself as both a religious and political leader in this new land. He founded a powerful mission, developed schools, printed documents, became an outspoken critic of slavery, re-introduced a secret society that opposed it and, even when forced to flee due to threats to his life, continued to advocate for assistance to tribesman loyal to the Union during the Civil War.

Although trials and tribulations followed his declining years, Jones efforts throughout a lifetime of service to the Cherokee did not go unnoticed or unappreciated. In death, as in life, his constituents trusted and revered him. Starr[6] quotes a powerful epitaph written following his death describing Jones stature and the esteem the Cherokee held for him:

> He was a man of scholarly attainments and acquired the Cherokee language and spoke it and wrote it freely. The confidence in which he was held among the Cherokees, who venerated him as a father, was never impaired. Even in the hours of his last illness, they came from far and near to hear a few last words of comfort in their native tongue from their revered friend. Cherokee Indian brethren...wept in deep sorrow while they remembered the virtues and deeds of their spiritual father.

What finer legacy could anyone leave than that?

Samuel Austin Worcester

Presbyterian Samuel Austin Worcester, ordained in 1825, was no stranger to men of the cloth, the family boasted seven generations of ministers. Born in 1778 in Worcester, Massachusetts, Samuel was the son of Leonard and Elizabeth Hopkins Worcester. He attended the University of Vermont where his namesake, Samuel Austin, was president. After graduating from the university in 1819, he attended Andover Theological Seminary where he met and married Ann Orr. Their marriage would produce seven children including a daughter, Ann Elizabeth. Samuel became a staunch supporter of the Cherokee and was a predominant settler in Indian Territory and even after his death the Worcester heritage continued to be deeply rooted in Oklahoma history. Many years later Ann Elizabeth's daughter, Alice Mary Robertson, would found Nuyaka Mission in Creek Indian Territory and in 1920 was elected as Oklahoma's first female representative to Congress.

Following his graduation from Andover and his ordination, Worcester applied to become a missionary for the American Board of Commissioners for Foreign Missions (ABCFM). He and Ann were assigned to Brainerd Mission in the Cherokee Nation. Immediately following their arrival in the summer of 1825 the couple began to learn and translate printed materials into the Cherokee language. In 1827 Samuel returned to Boston and purchased a printing press to publish the documents they were translating. The next year the couple was assigned to New Echota, the Cherokee capital and, with Elias Boudinot, began the necessary planning to print a newspaper, the *Cherokee Phoenix*. Boudinot became editor and Worcester was responsible for printing. The association resulted in a close friendship between the two lasting until Boudinot's assassination in Indian Territory in 1839. The paper was the first of its kind using the Cherokee syllabic alphabet developed by Sequoyah a few years earlier. It featured laws, documents and various Cherokee customs as well as the "news of the day." The first issue was published February 21, 1828, and, until it was shut down by the Georgia Military Guard in 1835, enabled those across the Nation to become more aware of current issues and events.

Worcester's involvement with printing the *Cherokee Phoenix* and Boudinot's editorials and articles demonstrated a partnership with missionaries and tribesmen that had not occurred before. This led tribal leaders to select an honorary Cherokee name for Worcester, A-tse-nu-st, meaning messenger. That would prove to be the first evidence of the high esteem held by the Cherokee for this New England Yankee but certainly not the last.

After Congress passed the Georgia Compact in 1802 promising to acquire all Indian lands within the state the friction between Georgia settlers, the federal government and the Cherokee leadership increased over the next two decades. The tribe historically had been divided into two factions, the Upper Towns and Lower Towns, and each had a different agenda. Upper Towns were more concerned about traditional issues while the Lower Towns were more focused on contemporary relationships with white settlers and issues with the Georgia government. But by 1827, the tribal agenda was consolidated when the two joined under one constitution patterned after the United States document. This unity further frustrated Georgians who now believed the Cherokee Tribe would be even more difficult to remove. In the meantime, white squatters continued to make incursions onto Cherokee lands, a situation that escalated substantially in 1829 when a virtual flood of settlers invaded northwest Georgia after gold was discovered. Mobilized by the increasing numbers of white settlers and their perceived need to resolve the issue of removal, Georgia legislators began developing restrictive laws and regulations. One law, presumably focusing on missionaries and their assistance to the tribe, required white people to obtain a license from the State when entering Cherokee Territory. Backed by the American Board of Commissioners for Foreign Missions (ABCFM) who believe this infringed on the rights of United

Samuel Austin Worcester

States citizens, eleven missionaries including Samuel Worcester published a resolution opposing the law and refused to obtain the license. They were arrested in April of 1831 and brought to trial in September. Nine of the imprisoned missionaries agreed to sign the necessary documents and accepted pardons after agreeing to leave the Nation. However, Worcester and Elizu Butler refused and were sentenced to four years at hard labor in the Milledgeville State Prison. With legal assistance from the ABCFM, an appeal entitled Worcester v. Georgia was heard by the United States Supreme Court, The judges disallowing the law ruling Georgia did not have jurisdiction over the Cherokee Nation as a sovereign entity, thus requiring Georgia to free the two men in 1832 after they had served sixteen months in prison. President Andrew Jackson, a firm advocate for the removal of all Indian Nations further west, refused to recognize the Supreme Court's decision and proceeded to promote ways and means that would lead to removal.

Worcester's courage and determination to confront the Georgia hierarchy on just one of what continued to be many repressive laws designed to uproot the Cherokee further endeared him to them. But those activities continued and, recognizing the inevitable in 1835 Samuel Worcester moved with his family joining Cephras Washburn at Dwight Mission in Indian Territory.

Continuing to pursue their focus on translation and publication, Samuel, Ann, the children and their printing press moved to Union Mission on the Grand River the next year. When Union was closed in 1836 they moved to Park Hill and established Park Hill Mission. The Fugate's[7] describe the mission compound as including, "...homes for missionaries and teachers, a boarding hall, gristmill, shops, stables, and a printing office and book bindery." Because of the focus on printing documents, that later included construction of the Cherokee Male and Female Seminaries, the Park Hill community became known regionally as "the Athens of the American Southwest."

Tragedy struck the Worcester household in 1839 when Ann

died during the birth of their last child, Mary Eleanor, and Elias Boudinot was assassinated for signing the Treaty of New Echota. To compound matters, the arrival of the Eastern Cherokee following the Trail of Tears resulted in considerable friction with the "Old Settlers," the Western Cherokee who had relocated to the region in 1828. Despite the personal tragedies that had befallen him and the inner tribal conflicts, Worcester worked tirelessly continuing to print documents, improve educational opportunities and mediate tribal differences. In April of 1841, Worcester married 39 year old Erminia Nash, a teacher from Dwight Mission. She was devoted to Samuel and the children. Wright[8] captures evidence of that devotion quoting the following from a letter Erminia wrote to the Worcester's youngest son John after he left for school in New England:

> I shall be very glad to get that letter when you have time-I want to know where you board & who washes & mends for you- where & how, with whom you lodge, & a great many things in relation to your comfort, & health. Give me the routine of a week, so that I may see a little how you are situated. Your affectionate Mother.

However, Erminia never regarded herself to be Samuel's equal, instead idolizing her husband from afar. In fact, Erminia's death bed request in 1872 was that she be buried at the foot of his grave because she didn't feel worthy to be buried beside him.

Samuel Austin Worcester died in 1859 at the age of 61 and is buried at the mission cemetery in Park Hill. A lasting reminder of the Worcester legacy remains in what once was New Echota in Georgia. During the Land Lottery of 1832 their home in New Echota was confiscated by a Georgian who obtained title to it. Acquired by the state of Georgia in 1952, it is the only remaining house in the former Cherokee capital.

Throughout his life with the Cherokee, Worcester astutely avoided involvement in the internal politics of the Nation, concentrating instead on defending their right as a sovereign nation as well as translating and printing the written word into Cherokee. As a result, the Cherokee frequently turned to him for objective advice and counsel on internal affairs.

Samuel Worcester's personal tragedies, imprisonment, the loss of his home in Georgia and the deaths of both his wife and best friend in 1839, seemed to galvanize him to become even more resolute in his contributions to the Cherokee. His legacy in the new Nation will continue to be the publications of thousands of printed documents that led to recognition of the Nation's focus on education. But his efforts to integrate white and Cherokee cultures may have been even more significant.

Jesse Bushyhead (Dta-ske-ge-de-hee)

Probably no member of the Cherokee Tribe became more respected for his ministry during his relatively brief life than did Jesse Bushyhead. Like many Cherokee, Jesse was born into a mixed race family and his unusual surname allegedly was acquired from his grandfather, Scotsman John Stuart. A popular British Indian agent, Stuart, was said to have a shock of red hair that led to tribesman referring to him as "Bushyhead," translated from the Cherokee language, and the surname was accepted by the family.

Born in 1804 near today's Cleveland in southeastern Tennessee to Stuart's only son Ol-no-du-tu, and Nancy Foreman a full blood Cherokee, Jesse, the oldest of seven children, was educated at Candy's Creek Mission. Later, he taught at several schools for boys and his skills as a teacher as well as his honesty and speaking ability engendered the trust of his fellow tribesmen. In 1830, at the age of 26 he was baptized and became a member of the Baptist Church. As an acquaintance of Baptist missionary Reverend Evan Jones, Bushyhead began assisting the preacher by translating his sermons into Cherokee. This association initiated a close relationship and later, through the forthcoming upheaval resulting in the removal of the tribe, the two became lifetime friends. Within two years of his conversion, Bushyhead's personal qualities and potential as a speaker were recognized and he was appointed assistant missionary by the Baptist Board of Foreign Missions. He is thought to be the second Cherokee so named.

Bushyhead married twice. The name of his first wife is unknown however the couple had two children. His second wife, Eliza Wilkerson or Wilkinson, bore him nine more. Many years later beginning in 1879, their eldest son, Dennis, would emulate his famous father's leadership and serve two terms as Principal Chief of the Cherokee Nation. Unfortunately the new Cherokee Nation would be deprived of the full potential of Jesse Bushyhead. Just a few years after his arrival in the new land he died after a short illness on July 17, 1843.

Following his conversion, Bushyhead's service to his church and community continued to result in growing confidence of his leadership. In 1837 he was among a small group chosen by John Ross and approved by the federal government to attempt to persuade the Seminoles to remove to Indian Territory. This confidence was also evidenced after the government began the forced removal of the Cherokee in 1838. As tensions escalated following the signing of the Treaty of New Echota more and more incidents began occurring involving Cherokee citizens, first between Georgia citizens and its militia, then federal troops. Homes were invaded without warning and families were imprisoned in open stockades with only the provisions they could carry. Livestock was driven off, household possessions stolen and the anguished protests of the owners were ignored by officials. Bushyhead, who also opposed the treaty, and his family were among those imprisoned. Rather than succumb to the same fate, many tribesmen and their families fled to the mountains.

Reacting to the threat of General Winfield Scott to hunt them down, and after the general agreed to wait until fall to initiate removal, Evan Jones and Bushyhead volunteered and were successful in persuading many of the refugees to return and make preparations to leave. He then agreed to lead one group of tribesmen from one of the more remote sections of the Nation. Conley[9] provides the following description of his contingent:

> The third wave was headed by Reverend Jesse Bushyhead. They left on September 3, 1838, and arrived on February 27, 1839. They were 178 days making the trip. Of the 950 who started the trip, 898 finished. Six births, thirty-eight deaths and 148 'desertions' were recorded.

Their journey led them north through Tennessee and Kentucky into Illinois where they crossed the Mississippi River near Cape Girardeau, Missouri, proceeding across the state of Arkansas to its western border.

Arriving in Indian Territory, he set to work with Jones establishing a place of worship and a distribution center for supplies about four miles north of today's Westville that soon became known as "Breadtown" to the arriving Cherokee contingents. Shortly thereafter the site included a church, school and trading post that became known as Baptist Mission. As the new arrivals disbursed throughout the Cherokee Nation, Jones, focused on the ministry at Baptist Mission and Bushyhead moved his family to a farm near the first Fort Wayne and present day Watts in Adair County.

Eager to return to his chosen vocation as a minister, as more tribesmen poured into the region, Bushyhead refused to be involved or intimidated by the inner tribal clash regarding the Treaty of New Echota. As sporadic violence or assassinations continued to occur he concentrated on his calling, preaching and traveling through small settlements and isolated meeting places as he often noted with pride, armed only with a Bible. In addition to his religious convictions, Jesse was a member of the Cherokee Temperance Society that strongly opposed the abuse of alcohol and he frequently organized meetings to convince

Jesse Bushyhead

others to avoid it. A strong supporter of the administration of John Ross, Bushyhead was also an abolitionist. He held several public offices. At the time of his death he was serving as Chief Justice of the Supreme Court for the Cherokee Nation.

Perhaps the most concise description of the man known as Jesse Bushyhead would be to say he led by example. From the time of his youth he was known for his honesty and integrity. As a teacher he gained considerable credibility among his fellow citizens. He was articulate and, after his appointment as assistant minister in the Baptist Church, became known as a gifted and articulate speaker. Although his loyalty was to the Ross Party, his sense of responsibility enabled him to reason with fellow tribesmen and accepting the inevitability of removal to Indian Territory. That was also reflected when he provided leadership to the new land for a contingent of mountain Cherokee that had no competent leader.

Bushyhead's impact upon the Cherokee Nation was summarized best by an outsider, U. S. Army Major General Ethan Allen Hitchcock. Foreman[10] notes Hitchcock's description:

> Jesse Bushyhead between 35 and 40 years of age – resides near old Fort Wayne, is of mixed blood – the Chief Justice of the Nation – a regular Baptist preacher – speaks English fluently and is considered the best interpreter in the Nation. He is universally respected and beloved. His mere opinion in the Nation has great weight and his persuasion upon almost any subject can win the people to his views. He is a fair minded man and if he can be satisfied, the Nation ought to acquiesce. If he is not satisfied, it may suggest a doubt whether some concessions may not be proper.

Jesse Bushyhead teacher, minister and public official, was recognized even by strangers as a man whose short life was well lived.

Stephen Foreman

Born near Rome, Georgia, on October 22, 1807, Stephen Foreman's life was in some ways typical of many biographical sketches presented in this book. Like so many Cherokee Foreman was of part Scotch ancestry, his father Anthony, a trader and businessman, married two Cherokee women. Susie (last name unknown) bore him six children before dying suddenly. Anthony was then married to Elizabeth, a niece of Susie's who also bore him six children including Stephen.

Education was important to the Foreman family just as it was for many and Stephen began attending school at the age of eight. Later, his father moved the family north into today's Bradley County, Tennessee where Stephen attended the Candy's Creek Mission School in 1824. Encouraged by William Holland one of the school's founders, four years later he left the school to study with Reverend Samuel Worcester in New Echota.

Appointed assistant editor of the *Cherokee Phoenix* in 1829, his work was so impressive that Worcester recommended him for the ministry. He studied both in Virginia and later at Princeton Theological Seminary in New Jersey. After finishing his studies he returned in 1832 and was assigned to teach at his former school, Candy's Creek. He was ordained as a Presbyterian minister in 1835.

The year before his ordination Foreman married Sarah Watkins Riley and the couple had three children, Austin, Ermina, and Jeremiah who was born during the journey west on the Trail of Tears. Ermina, became a teacher and was assigned to Dwight Mission. Later in 1841, she married Samuel Worcester following the death of his first wife Ann two years earlier.

Like so many influential citizens of his time, Foreman became involved in the Cherokee political affairs taking place and he chose to support the efforts of John Ross and the Nationalist Party to overturn the Treaty of New Echota. He was selected as a committee delegate to Washington to attempt to persuade officials to reject the treaty. Their efforts eventually failed by one vote in the United States Senate and the impetus to begin removal of the Cherokee Tribe began.

The events that followed have been reviewed previously, homes and possessions were seized, families imprisoned in makeshift open air "forts," stockades guarded by Georgia militia or United States soldiers and this included the Stephen Foreman family. During the spring and summer of 1838 they were incarcerated in Camp Aquohee, one of a number of hastily constructed compounds that provided no supplies or accommodations other than those carried from their homes by the detainees. Open to the weather with no provision for sanitation or other basic human needs, many died.

General Winfield Scott, in command of approximately 7,000 troops, enforced the order to evacuate the Nation and, during May of 1838, began the removal of approximately 3,000 Cherokee under guard. That effort proved to be disastrous and, after Chief Ross negotiated an agreement for voluntary removal, activities were delayed until fall. Members of the Cherokee leadership were recruited to lead contingents and Stephen Foreman and Captain John Oldfield were among those selected Their detachment of 950 left on October 20, 1838, and reached Indian Territory February 27, 1839, concluding a journey of 153 days.

After their arrival the Foremans were attracted to the Park Hill community, founded four years earlier in 1834. His friend and mentor Samuel Worcester, who left Georgia earlier, established a mission at Park Hill in 1836 and shortly thereafter also began printing a variety of religious and educational materials. Selecting a site for their new home, the Foreman residence was built between the Worcester's and another friend, Elias Boudinot, former publisher of the *Cherokee Phoenix.*

In addition to his calling as a minister and assisting Worcester with printing documents, Foreman was again recruited into public service. He was designated as a member of the Select Committee established to organize a government and devise a means to address relationship issues with the "Old Settlers" as well as the rift between Traditionalists and Treaty Signers. But a later assignment as superintendent of a common school system may well have resulted in his most outstanding contribution to the new nation.

True to the general interest in education within the Cherokee Tribe, in December, 1841, the National Council approved the school system, thought to be the first west of the Mississippi. As superintendent he immediately went to work supervising construction of schools in the various districts and selecting teachers. According to Faulkner[11] in a letter dated July 5, 1843, Foreman reports, "During the last year, (1842) ten out of eleven schools were in successful operation and something over 400 children were collected and received instructions in several of the elementary branches of education."

Initiating an elementary system wasn't Foreman's only accomplishment. In 1851, seminaries were opened for older students, both males and females. The buildings, faculty and curriculum rivaled those of elite schools back east. In addition to traditional subjects, students in advanced placement classes could enroll in, among others, Greek, Intellectual Philosophy, Xenophone's Anabasis or Rhetoric. Unfortunately, the tribal government had not developed a system of taxation necessary to support them and the seminaries were forced to close five years later because of lack of funds.

The onset of the Civil War proved both disappointing and devastating to Foreman. He became disillusioned with John Ross, who after agreeing to support the Confederate cause, became closely associated with Evan Jones and the Keetoowah Society. His concerns were justified when both Ross and Society members joined Union forces and fled North in the summer of 1862. However, he became even more distraught when he himself was apparently targeted for death. After several narrow encounters and fearing for both his family and himself, Foreman fled to Texas for the remainder of the war.

Stephen Foreman

Returning to Park Hill following the war, Foreman and his family attempted to resume life in their war torn country. Even through the devastation and ensuing lawlessness he continued his work at the Park Hill Mission until finally it was closed for lack of funds in 1878. Stephen Foreman died December 8, 1881, but his passing drew well deserved accolades. His services to the Cherokee Nation, according to Faulkner, were recognized by the National Council as "a zealous defender of all that is pure, good, and noble in human society."

Like so many of his peers, it is difficult to identify just one outstanding accomplishment in the lifetime of Stephen Foreman. As he matured he addressed several different issues. Early on he became a successful interpreter and journalist, later he was chosen to join in efforts to overturn the Treaty of New Echota and, when that failed he assisted in leading a contingent of fellow citizens to the new Indian Territory. Foreman's own existence in the new nation continued to serve as an example to others. He maintained journalistic and ministerial responsibilities and assisted with governmental issues through appointment on several committees. But perhaps his most notable contribution was his effort to establish a school system that was the forerunner of common education in Oklahoma today.

BIBLIOGRAPHY

[1]Breen, Nakai. *The Ancient Religious Beliefs of the Cherokee People.* Internet. http://cherokeenationofSequoyah.com/ancientbeliefs.html. March, 2015.

[2]Foreman, Grant. *Indian Removal.* University of Oklahoma Press. Norman. 1932. P. 286, P. 296.

[3]The Trail of Tears Association, Oklahoma Chapter. *The Journal of Rev. Daniel S. Butrick.* Original at Houghton Library, Harvard University, Cambridge, MA. The Trail of Tears Association. Park Hill, OK. 1998. P.1, P33.

[4]Holway, Hope. *Union Mission, 1826-1837.* Chronicles of Oklahoma. Oklahoma Historical Society. Vol. 40-4. 1962 P. 356, P. 372.

[5]McDermott, John P., Editor. *Western Journals of Washington Irving.* University of Oklahoma Press. 1944.

[6]Starr, Emmett. *History of the Cherokee Indians.* Hoffman Printing Company. Muskogee, OK. 1984. P. 255-256.

[7]Fugate, Francis L. and Roberta B. *Roadside history of Oklahoma.* Mountain Press Publishing Company. Missoula, MT. 1991. P. 32.

[8]Wright, Muriel H. *Samuel Austin Worcester: A Dedication.* Chronicles of Oklahoma. Vol. 37-1. Oklahoma Historical Society. P. 20.

[9]Conley, Robert J. *The Cherokee Nation, A History.* University of New Mexico Press. Albuquerque. 2005. P. 155.

[10]Foreman, Grant. *A Traveler in Indian Territory.* University of Oklahoma Press. Norman. 1995. P. 233.

[11]Faulkner, Cooleela. *The Life and Times of Reverend Stephen*

Foreman. Cherokee Heritage Press. Tahlequah, Oklahoma. 2006. p. 209, P. 195.

CHAPTER 6

Nation Builders

A fter a few tumultuous years the Traditionalists, Treaty
Signers and Western Cherokees, who relocated
from western Arkansas Territory in 1828, eventually
began to work together. They established a government, a
judiciary, developed a school system and citizens were engaged
in productive farming and a variety of commercial endeavors.
By 1850, the bitter dispute caused by the signing of the Treaty
of New Echota in Georgia had toned down somewhat. From
all outward appearances, the founding fathers were on track to
fulfill the vision of a new and robust Cherokee Nation.

A "backfill" of settlement occurred during this time involving
both legitimate Indian citizens and illegitimate squatters. Earlier,
even before the Trail of Tears, scattered settlements occurred
as far north as the Timber Hill region in today's eastern Craig
and western Ottawa Counties and as far west as the Verdigris
River in the future Rogers County. Out of necessity trails
became roads, supplies were needed and gristmills were built
to accommodate these early pioneers. This combination led to
the eventual formation of a network of towns and communities
scattered throughout the Nation developed within reasonable
distance to serve the isolated farms and ranches.

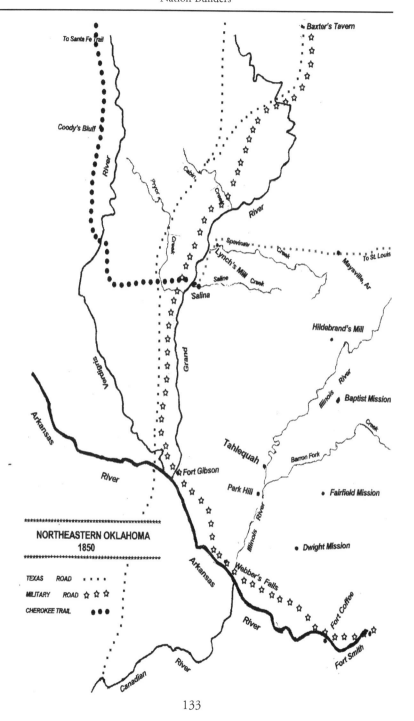

To Santa Fe Trail

Baxter's Tavern

Coody's Bluff

River

Cabin

Creek

River

Spavinaw

Creek

To St. Louis

Maysville, Ar

Lynch's Mill

Saline

Creek

Salina

Hildebrand's Mill

Illinois

River

Baptist Mission

Creek

Grand

Tahlequah

Barron Fork

Verdigris

Fairfield Mission

Fort Gibson

Park Hill

Illinois

River

Arkansas

River

Dwight Mission

NORTHEASTERN OKLAHOMA
1850

Arkansas

Webber's Falls

TEXAS ROAD

Fort Coffee

MILITARY ROAD

CHEROKEE TRAIL

River

Fort Smith

Canadian

River

133

Even as the Cherokee were moving into the territory, a rush of white settlers started through shortly after 1820, traveling south on what became known as the Texas Road. It consisted of two branches on either side of the Grand River that merged at Salina before continuing to Texas, one route from St. Louis the other from settlements north through Baxter Springs. The Texas Road became the "super highway of its era when Moses Austin, and later his son, Steven, negotiated an almost unbelievable arrangement with the Mexican government to encourage the settlement of Texas in the Brazos River country. Families could obtain over 4,000 acres for $30.00, payable within six years! The result was a virtual stampede of over 25,000 settlers within the next two decades most traveling by wagon from the United States southwest across Indian Territory. Foreman[1] quotes from an official report about the St. Louis route submitted by a Lieutenant J. W. Abert, as he returned from Fort Gibson:

> The way from Fort Gibson was literally lined with wagons of emigrants to Texas and from this time until we arrived at Saint Louis, we continued daily to see hundreds of them.

A second road, the Military Road, was surveyed and opened in 1837 as a frontier defense mechanism that was patrolled by the newly formed Dragoon companies. It eventually extended from Minnesota to Louisiana and was heavily traveled like the Texas Road. One stop was at the Martin ranch at Cabin Creek where stage coaches changed, lodging was available and supplies could be obtained. The traffic would not soon diminish. When gold was discovered in California in 1849, many used them both on their way west to either connect with the California Road that paralleled the Cimarron River, or to routes further south.

The influx of Texas or California bound pioneers also introduced others to the potential of Northeastern Oklahoma and some stayed either as illegal squatters or becoming legitimate by marrying Cherokee women and farming or developing businesses in communities. The complexion of the Nation became a combination of full blood Indians, mixed bloods, and an overwhelming number of white settlers. Within just 60 years, by 1900, the national census would reflect that within the Indian Nations, at least half were Caucasian.

This influx began early on. In addition to Chouteau's early trading post at La Saline, and Bogy's at Three Forks, other mixed settlements soon followed including the founding of several missions and Cantonment (later Fort) Gibson in 1824. They were joined by the community of Agency Landing, located on the west bank of the Arkansas near the confluence of the three rivers. Shortly after 1828, when the Western Cherokee relocated to initiate the Cherokee Nation west, Talontuskee and Webbers Falls were founded. From that time forward mills, country stores and, after the middle of the 18th Century, even watering stops for locomotives became the nexus that saw towns and cities emerge.

While settlements were developing, the concept of herding longhorn cattle from southern Texas to profitable markets in the north and east was also gaining momentum. The Texas Longhorn, a crossbreed between Spanish Criollos and English cattle needed only grass to survive. Extremely hardy animals, they could endure heat and extreme cold, swim rivers and survive droughts. At ten cents on the dollar, rounding them up and selling them in northern cities was very profitable. After Edward Piper successfully herded cattle from southern Texas and sold them in Cincinnati, Ohio, in 1840, others lured by such a profitable venture became involved. The Texas Road, utilized by pioneers traveling south beginning in the 1820s, became known as the Shawnee Trail for vast herds of cattle headed north in the 1840s. In places it was nearly a mile wide, the clay packed by hooves and wagon wheels. The cattlemen's name for the northbound trail supposedly came from a Shawnee village located on the Texas side of the Red River. It has been estimated, excluding the four years of Civil War, that by 1866, perhaps a million Longhorns crossed the region, south to north. After that, since

Northeastern Oklahoma was becoming so populated with farms and communities, and railroads were penetrating Kansas territory, trail bosses began using routes from Texas further west across the less populated area later to become known as Oklahoma Territory.

The introduction of railroads ultimately proved to be both good news and bad news for the fledgling Cherokee Nation. The decision by the Cherokee leadership to join the confederate cause ultimately backfired providing an opportunity after the war for the United States Congress to cease the formality of constructive negotiations and begin issuing mandates. That attitude first became evident when, following the war, the federal government's focus was on restoring the south, completely ignoring the devastation that occurred in the Cherokee Nation. In the fall of 1865 a delegation was dispatched from Washington and after several contentious meetings, another treaty finally was negotiated but required ratification in Washington. After still more meetings were conducted at the capitol a treaty was signed in 1866 that included forcing the Cherokee Nation to grant railroad rights-of-way, the right to establish United States courts within the Nation, and the right to establish military posts if necessary. Land in Kansas including the Neutral Land and the Cherokee Strip was also ceded to the United States. No such demands were made of southern states. In retrospect, particularly the granting of railroad rights-of-way and establishing courts would mark the beginning of the end of the Cherokee Nation. Railroads would bring more Caucasians and the United States would add courts, a second law enforcement entity, within the Nation primarily to adjudicate them. As noted earlier, by 1900 the Indian Nations were approximately 50% white.

If the Treaty of 1866 was not sufficient to contribute to the demise of the Cherokee Nation, beginning in 1870 and for the next twenty years, a constant barrage of bills were introduced in congress to convert Indian Territory into one or more states. But it would be the action of the Dawes Committee overturning the

Indian concept of "land held in common" that would ultimately destroy the strict sovereignty of the Cherokee Nation. In 1893 a bill was passed appointing a commission, soon known as the Dawes Commission for Chairman Henry Dawes. According to Carter[2] the commission was "to negotiate the extinguishment of the national or tribal title to land either by cession or allotment in severalty," legal speak for dividing and allocating the land by acre and section.

The first railroad, thc Kansas, Missouri and Texas (Katy) reached Northeastern Oklahoma in 1871 from the north and the Union Pacific from the east. The Katy construction stretched from Chetopah, Kansas to Denton, Texas and was completed in little over a year. (The Union Pacific stopped at Vinita in 1871, continuing after Tulsa was incorporated in 1882.) Other spur lines would eventually cross the region providing a network connecting towns and villages with the main line routes. The result was a phenomenal boost in agricultural production by enabling heavy farm machinery to be shipped in and a variety of farm products to be shipped out.

It would be inaccurate to assume that because the vestiges of civilization, railroads and more settlers arriving that a greater population toned down the violence that plagued the region since its first settlement. The conflicting laws that governed Indian citizens and those covering white settlers provided ample opportunity for rampant crime and occasional repentance. One Pathfinder who was repentant, Zeke Proctor, is presented as an example of a converted Nation Builder. Another, Ned Christie, was not and has arguably been branded both a criminal and patriot. Most of that element remained as hardened criminals who made existence for the average citizen during the later years of the 19th century just as precarious as in earlier times. Although many outlaws were "shot on the spot," the capture and demise of a few who terrorized Northeastern Oklahoma and paid the ultimate price in Judge Parker's court under the supervision of hangman George Maldone are summed up by Shirley[3]:

1873 – James Diggs murdered cattle drover J. C. Gould for $27 near the Kansas line.

1875 – William Leach murdered John Wadkins an itinerant minstrel who hired Leach to show him the road to Fayetteville. A month later a hunter discovered his charred bones and the skull with a bullet hole.

1875 – Osee Sanders killed Thomas S. Carlyle for $1,200 and was apprehended the next day.

1881 – Edward Fulsom beat William Massingill to death with a pistol near the Arkansas–Indian Territory line.

1883 – William Phillips murdered his father-in-law in bed.

1883 – Kit Ross shot Jonathan Davis outside a store in Chouteau.

1886 – John Stephens murdered Annie Kerr with an axe. She had testified against him in a trial.

1886 – While in camp Patrick McCarty murdered the Mahoney brothers with an axe.

1887 – Owen Hill who lived near Gibson Station slit his wife's throat with a razor nearly cutting her head off.

1896 – Crawford Goldsby, alias Cherokee Bill, the most vicious member of the infamous Cook Gang took part in robberies and murders that were unprecedented even for that era.

Crimes and criminal deeds continued well into the early 20th century. While progress was made, this segment of Indian Territory continued to contain many vestiges of the lawless frontier even after statehood and then again in the 1930s when crime surged regionally and across the Nation born by the winds of depression.

In summary, circumstances seemingly beyond anyone's control eventually led to the demise of the Cherokee Nation as a sovereign entity. Surrounded by other states, all of Indian Territory would eventually become enveloped by a government that for over a century used every means at hand to eradicate the unique identity of Native Americans. But the transition was met with either fierce resistance or exemplified by men who, in good faith, attempted to create a new Nation or contribute to its infrastructure.

Joseph Lynch Martin

Possibly the wealthiest man in the Cherokee Nation prior to the Civil War, Joe Martin oversaw 100,000 acres of land, a total of 156 square miles. During the two decades prior to the Civil War the ranch was in operation, Martin acquired a portion of his wealth from rounding up cattle that strayed from Texas herds driven north. He and his slaves would drive the cattle and sell them at either Kansas City or St. Joseph, Missouri frequently at $100 dollars a head. He also sold teams of oxen for a reputed $100 dollars a pair to west-bound pioneers after the slaves fashioned yokes for them. According to one source[4] over a period of time "he sold 700 teams of oxen to settlers on the way west."

Joseph Lynch Martin was born August 20, 1820 to John and Nellie Martin on a plantation along Sautee Creek in Georgia. He received his education at the Virginia Military Institute. His father was appointed as a circuit judge on the Cherokee Tribal Court and also served as treasurer until 1837 when, due to the unrest in the Cherokee Nation, he led 300 Cherokee to Indian Territory and settled near present day Locust Grove. The elder Martin was elected as the first Chief Justice of the Cherokee Supreme Court in 1839 and undoubtedly had considerable influence on Joe's ability to acquire land in Indian Territory. Under Cherokee law, land could be leased and used but not owned outright and young Martin accumulated his land rights for ½ cent per acre.

In 1839 Joe married Julia Lombard[5]. Over a period of 30 years he would marry four more times because childbirth and the ravages of disease affecting women of the era would be particularly

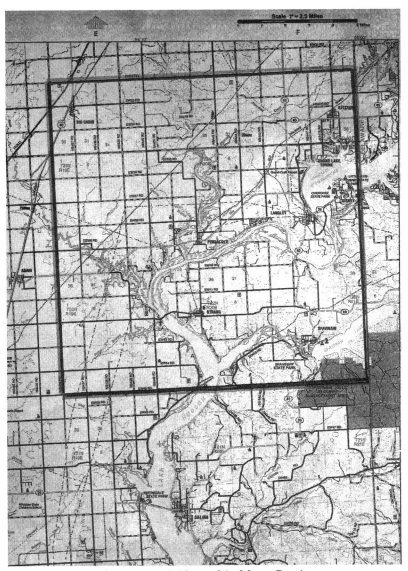

Approximate holdings of the Martin Ranch

Joseph Martin

devastating to the Martin family. After their marriage the couple constructed a home known as Greenbrier that overlooked the Grand River east of the present day Greenbrier Baptist Church on EW44 Road in Mayes County. The home was located on the southern edge of what would become his vast land holdings. Martin apparently chose the name in recognition of Greenbrier, West Virginia, the home of the Martin ancestral family. He also personally acquired the name "Greenbrier Joe" because of that connection.

Julia died in 1845 leaving him a widower with two children and in 1847 Joe married Sallie Childers. Shortly after building Greenbrier and as his land holdings and wealth expanded, Martin constructed a second residence and several outbuildings along the Texas Road at the Cabin Creek crossing that he named Pensacola. The Texas Road passed within a few miles of Greenbrier further south, but it literally passed the front door of the Pensacola home at Cabin Creek. The large two story frame home would witness a considerable amount of history from a variety of perspectives before it burned in 1906.

Martin's construction at Pensacola, the home and other plantation buildings, was by design. Beginning in the early 1830s the Texas Road became the major thorough fare through Northeastern Oklahoma for pioneers traveling to Texas to acquire land. Steven Austin had negotiated an almost unbelievable land deal with Mexican authorities who wanted to colonize Texas. After gaining its freedom from Mexico, Texas became a state in 1846, and traffic increased even more dramatically. That surge was followed by the California gold rush in 1849. Historians have estimated that as many as 100,000 wagons used the Texas Road during this period, all passing through Pensacola. As a result, Pensacola became a virtual commercial gold mine. Nearly all of the wagon traffic traveled south. After leaving Baxter Springs, Kansas, the sixty mile drive to Cabin Creek and Pensacola became an important intermediate destination for pioneers. Seizing on the opportunity, Martin provided necessary services such as replenishing supplies for travelers, feed for animals and maintaining a blacksmith shop for needed repairs. Given the volume of customers and the fees he charged, his wealth grew dramatically. Later, Pensacola was also an overnight stop for the Chittenson Stage Coach Line whose travelers boarded at Baxter Springs and stayed at Knell's Tavern near the Pensacola compound before proceeding to Fort Gibson and Fort Smith the next morning.

All of these services required manpower and Martin increasingly acquired more slaves to work the land. In addition to the periodic cattle drives north and providing services at Pensacola he also raised cotton and corn on the river bottoms and cattle on the prairie. The exact number of slaves Martin possessed is subject to debate and estimates vary. Family sources indicate that on one trip to New Orleans, Martin allegedly purchased 103 slaves at one time. Historians have verified that there were a large number of slave cabins south of the Cabin Creek home along both sides of the Texas Road although neither the precise number of buildings nor the number of occupants is known. He was said to have treated them "firmly but fair." That was demonstrated at least in one instance as when the two Civil War battles were approaching at Cabin Creek in 1863 and 1864, Martin ordered his slaves to leave and protect themselves. Later, when the war was over and the slaves were freed, many came back to his plantations, but Martin was destitute and there was no work.

During the war both Martin, who became a major and quartermaster, and his 17 year old son Richard, served under the command of Confederate General Stand Watie, participating among others in both battles at Cabin Creek. Martin witnessed the destruction of many buildings at Pensacola first hand. But this was not his most significant war-time loss. Like many affluent Cherokee, when the war began Martin evacuated his wife Sallie and the younger children south and out of harm's way. Tragedy struck the Martin family again as in 1863, Sallie died in the Choctaw Nation. Over the years six more children had been born to that union and Joe was again a widower. Soon after the war Martin married Lucy Rogers but shortly after the birth of a daughter, Joanna, Lucy also passed away. During the remaining years of his life, Joe would marry two more times, to Caroline Garrett who bore four children and Jennie Harlan, who, after bearing three children, survived Joe living 15 years following Martin's death. Consequently, it is little wonder that the Martin name is common place in Northeastern Oklahoma. In fact, the Martin descendants hold a family reunion annually each fall at Spavinaw near the site where Joe once owned a grist mill in the 1840s and 50s.

Following the war, Joseph Lynch Martin spent his declining years at Greenbrier after rebuilding it. The ravages of war that permeated Northeastern Oklahoma affected Martin as well. With no slaves to operate what had once been his vast estate, the rapid decline of the traffic on the Texas Road, particularly with the advent of the railroads in Indian Territory in 1871 and cattle now hauled by rail, Pensacola and the ranch holdings soon dissolved. Joe, like his fellow Cherokee Nation survivors, eked out a living at Greenbrier until his death in 1891.

At some point following his loss, the hard driving entrepreneur and task master, the Civil War officer who fought with General Stand Watie from the beginning until the end, demonstrated another creative side to his personality. For several years he submitted articles on various subjects and an occasional poem to the *Cherokee Advocate* printed in Tahlequah. One of the last, composed seven months before his death was entitled "Stanza's by Uncle Joe."[6]

After identifying three nieces Ellen, Ann and Cherokee then describing each, Martin concludes:

> I Love you Children, oh so well!
> Better far than ever I can tell.
> The reason I love you so good,
> Is because in your veins runs my blood.

The life of Joseph Lynch Martin is a reflection of many that settled Northeastern Oklahoma. His background was one of wealth and privilege not uncommon among many mixed blood Cherokee who migrated to Indian Territory. But only a few could match his accomplishments after the family settled near present day Locust Grove. The 19 year old Martin married, than immediately began efforts to develop and expand his holdings. While the home at Greenbrier marked both his first efforts and eventually became his retreat after the war, constructing Pensacola at a site on the Texas Road proved to be a stroke of genius that enabled him to reach unprecedented heights with a 100,000 acre ranch and the resources it provided. Perhaps if the war had not occurred that destroyed his dream, Joseph Martin would be noted in Oklahoma history for developing the first ranch of its size in the state, his contributions to the commerce of that era and after the war, his uplifting and philosophical attitude despite the circumstances.

Elias Cornelius Boudinot

Elias Cornelius Boudinot, (E.C.) son of Elias Boudinot (Galigina) and Harriet Ruggles Gold, was born August 1, 1835, in New Echota, Cherokee Nation East. His mother was the daughter of the influential Gold family living in Cornwell, Connecticut, and, when the marriage of his father, an Indian to a white woman, was announced in 1826, there was considerable consternation within the Cornwell community. Confronted with this discrimination, the young couple moved almost immediately to the Cherokee Nation East.

Within months after the birth of E.C., his father Elias became one of a small group of Cherokee that approved the controversial Treaty of New Echota granting land claimed by the Nation to the United States government. The event created such a volatile climate for those that signed, most soon moved to Indian Territory. Unfortunately, in addition to the upheaval involving the signing, the summer following the signing, Harriet died of complications resulting from the death of a still born child. Tragic circumstances continued to haunt the family After moving to Park Hill in Indian Territory, three years later in June of 1839, E.C.'s father Elias was assassinated during a coordinated conspiracy to kill several who signed the treaty. Because of the violent death of their father and fearing further retribution, the Boudinot children, including four year old E.C., were sent to Connecticut to be reared by their grandparents, the Gold family.

Growing to manhood young Boudinot first studied civil engineering, then law and was admitted to the bar in 1856 at the age of 21. He established his practice in Fayetteville, Arkansas. In 1861 he was appointed secretary of the Arkansas Secession Convention while the state leadership deliberated whether or not to join the Confederacy before the Civil War. When the decision was made to join, he was elected to be a delegate to the Confederate Congress and later obtained the rank of Lieutenant Colonel in the Cherokee Rifles, serving under his uncle Stand Watie.

Following the war and now just 30 years old, then returning to Washington, E.C. began a 20 year career as an attorney and many of his clients were prominent railroad officials. He also was involved in land acquisition for western railroad development and promoted the successful construction of the Missouri, Kansas & Texas (Katy) railroad in 1871. He became popular with Washington politicians because he advocated for the opening of unassigned Indian lands in western and southwestern Oklahoma to white settlement. But he became a subject of controversy among his own people when he argued that Indians should become citizens of the United States in order to be protected by the Constitution. Boudinot also believed that Indian lands should be held by individual title rather than through the ancient custom of joint tribal ownership.

Elias Cornelius Boudinot

While E.C. was successful in his activities in Washington he was not so fortunate in business efforts at home. In 1868 he joined in partnership with Stand Watie to construct a tobacco factory near the Arkansas border reasoning that Arkansas citizens would be especially supportive because there was no excise tax charged on products in Indian Territory. However, the federal government sued over the tax issue and the Supreme Court ruled against him stating Congress had the authority to change previous treaty agreements.

During his tenure in Washington the charismatic bachelor had a lengthy relationship with famed artist Vinnie Ream whose sculptures of prominent Washington dignitaries gave her considerable visibility. Although the relationship did not end in marriage, in 1871 he was involved in renaming Downingville, located near the Katy railroad, Vinita in her honor. In 1885, at the age of 50, E.C. married Clara Minear in Washington. The couple moved to Fort Smith where he established a law practice and operated a ranch nearby. His life was cut short when he contracted dysentery and died September 27, 1890.

The life of E. C. Boudinot is a study in contrasts. Although born in the Cherokee Nation, E.C. grew up in white society and was educated in New England. As a young lawyer in Arkansas he quickly rose to prominence as a politician advocating for Cherokee support of the Confederacy and being appointed to important diplomatic positions. Following the Civil War he was instrumental in obtaining some favorable terms of peace for fellow Cherokee tribesman.

However, after becoming a seasoned lawyer in Washington he advocated for issues contrary to the belief of most Cherokee including tribesmen obtaining United States citizenship instead of maintaining the sovereignty of the Nation, promoting the Homestead Act as a means of settling unassigned Indian lands, as well as advancing the concept of owning land by individual title. As years passed and while disconnected with the tribe he lobbied for railroads and became immersed in Washington society. Still, near the end of his life this brilliant attorney chose to return to his roots and died among his fellow tribesmen. Whether or not he could have used his intellect and political connections to assist in addressing more post war issues in the Cherokee Nation will remain a subject for debate among historians.

Robert Smith Stevens

Robert "Bob" Stevens is one example of a Nation Builder whose contribution was extremely important but tenure was brief. He was born March 27, 1824, in Attica, New York, the son of Alden and Aschsa Smith. Bob became a school teacher in 1844 and also studied to become a lawyer. He was admitted to the bar in 1846 and in 1852 married his distant cousin, Mary Proctor Smith. The couple had one son, Fredrick.

In 1856 the Stevens moved to Lecompton, Kansas, the territorial capitol, and two years later he was appointed mayor then served two years in the Kansas State Senate. Stevens, a democrat, supported James Buchanan for president and following his election was appointed special commissioner to arrange property sales for land deeded to the United States by several tribes in Kansas who had been overrun by white squatters.

He moved to Lawrence in 1862 and became president of a local bank. Perhaps the most dramatic experience of Steven's life was when he narrowly escaped death during the raid on Lawrence during August of 1863 when a gang conducted a surprise raid on the town. Known as Quantrill's Raiders, they succeeded in killing 123, making every effort to burn the town to the ground. Bob Stevens escaped by hiding along the bank of a nearby creek. Quantrill and his gang became infamous for similar deeds until he was finally killed in 1864.

This rising star obviously was in a position for achieving greater accomplishments and the opportunity occurred in 1869 when financial backers won a contract to supervise construction of the

Robert Stevens

Missouri, Kansas and Texas (Katy) railroad in an attempt to be the first railroad to reach the Kansas and Cherokee territorial border. Congress had determined that the first railroad, one from the north and one from the east, would be permitted to build tracks across the Cherokee Nation.

Stevens was appointed head of construction and general manager and was ably assisted by John Scullin. Scullin, tough and knowledgeable, had previously acquired extensive experience managing the incorrigible Irishmen who made up many of the railroad construction crews after the Civil War. Work on the Katy began at Fort Riley, Kansas, during the summer of 1869 and the rails that were laid generally followed the Neosho River, eventually covering 182 miles to Chetopa on the border of the Cherokee Nation. Other competitors were the Leavenworth, Lawrence and Fort Gibson and the Border Tier Railroads. Eventually, the former posed no threat to the Katy, but the Border Tier actually reached Indian Territory first, just south of Baxter Springs, but it proved to be the wrong Indian Territory! The Border Tier Railroad which had been constructed south from Fort Scott following the Kansas–Missouri border through Baxter Springs and reached the boundary of the Quapaw Nation. Congress had given specific approval for a railroad to cross, north and south, but to the Cherokee Nation. In order to resolve the dilemma, the Border Tier construction workers would be required to build track west for 17 miles before being able to cross south into the Cherokee Nation. Time would not permit it and the Katy won by default. During June, 1870, the Katy arrived at the Cherokee Nation border 20 miles west of Baxter Springs. Concluding a short ceremony, E. C. Boudinot, who previously lobbied in Washington on behalf of the Katy, was given the honor of driving the first spike in Cherokee territory.

As construction proceeded south there were frequent delays due to the lack of materials and the working conditions proved to be even more difficult. Enterprising Indians fenced large portions of wooded areas and, when wooden ties were needed, charged exorbitant prices for them. Rails and spikes were frequently in short supply. Unforeseen working conditions occurred. Masterson[7] reports one conversation between Stevens and Scullin involving the hordes of insects the crews encountered:

> It was utterly impossible to do work on the prairie during the day, Stevens was told. The stock was nearly eaten up alive. Scullin had his horses and mules covered entirely over with burlaps, he had made leggings for them and rubbed every exposed portion of their flesh with fish oil, yet blood fairly dripped from them at times, it was reported.

Working conditions were often deplorable. Masterson also notes:

> Before they could do their jobs they had to cut and slash their way through countless malaria-infested bottoms, etc.

And there were issues with camp followers. As development progressed, growing numbers of thieves, prostitutes and dishonest merchants did everything possible to relieve construction crew members of their wages.

After track was laid across the Three Forks to Muskogee, neither steamboats that previously ascended the Arkansas River, nor supply wagons following the Texas Road were now the essential commercial link between Northeastern Oklahoma and the rest of the nation. Both were rapidly being replaced by railroads. Communities emerged beside them, often initially created by water tanks necessary to replenish locomotives or because switches were built to load box cars. Towns such as Welch, Vinita, Adair, Wagoner and others emerged because of those water tanks and railroad switches. The new communities were now linked to the most modern travel venue available. Stage coach's carrying passengers or commerce moved by wagons were reduced to linking distant rural communities to these rail sites. Cattle drives to northern markets were suspended, now shipped more efficiently by rail. Mercantile goods, previously unavailable on the frontier, could now be shipped almost anywhere. Farmers acquired heavy, horse drawn equipment that previously could not be obtained so farms grew and production expanded. Because of the Katy railroad and the Union Pacific being built from east to west, the region had taken a giant step in becoming more integrated nationally as well as being more economically productive.

Unlike other Nation Builders who spent years in the region, Bob Stevens only stayed during the duration of the construction of the Katy Railroad. But from the standpoint of expanding commercially, the impact of his contribution and that of his colleagues must be considered to be of significant importance in the development of the region. Opposed by the Cherokee National Council because construction of the railroad threatened their sovereignty, fraught with adverse conditions of nature and continually corralling his unruly work force, Stevens found a way to construct the railway in a matter of months. It opened the territory to the most modern method of travel available, connected it to markets and enabled local agricultural production to soar.

But not all of the Katy's impact was positive. It also substantially increased the number of white settlers that, in turn would see more involvement by the federal government in the Cherokee Nation. And the resulting wave of crime underscored the fact that not all were upstanding citizens, a problem that multiplied the difficulty of law enforcement and reopened the argument about which entity had jurisdiction. In perspective, the railroad brought both problems and contemporary trends to the region. After completion of the Katy, Bob Stevens continued in the business of railroad construction until 1879 when he returned to his birth place, Attica, New York. After serving one term in the United States House of Representatives in 1883, he retired and died ten years later.

Matthias Splitlog

Reports vary on the origins of young Matthias Splitlog who became known as "the Indian Millionaire." One version suggests that he was born in 1812 in New York State to a French father and Cayuga mother. Another is that he was of French-Canadian descent and was stolen by Wyandotte Indians as a baby and a third contends that Matthias was a Canadian-Mohawk Indian. Regardless, of his early background, it is apparent that as a youngster he lived with the Wyandotte Tribe in Ohio, married Eliza Charloe Barnett and, because of this marriage became a member of the Wyandotte Tribe. Four boys and two girls were born to this union.

Because of his unusual title as "the Indian Millionaire," it is important to provide background information on how he obtained his wealth. When the tribe was removed to Kansas in 1843, the Splitlog family moved with them and initially located on a portion of land along the Neosho River designated by the United States government. Several tribal leaders found the tract to be unsatisfactory and purchased 39 sections of land at the fork of the Missouri and Kansas (or Kaw) rivers which fortuitously later would become Kansas City. Land further east of that site had been occupied by white settlers for some time. Francois Chouteau opened a trading post near a bend on the Missouri River known as Chouteau's landing in 1821 and further south in 1833 John McCoy established a site known as Westport. Westport was in the early stages of becoming the eastern terminal for pioneers who eventually departed west on the Santa Fe, Oregon or California trails.

The Splitlogs relocated on the new site on a hill overlooking the two rivers and their new purchase proved to be an excellent choice. Matthias built a log home on the land and later exhibiting the first of his innate engineering skills, built a grist mill and saw mill on the site, both powered by steam. By 1853 the area including Westport, the Chouteau site, and Splitlog's land was

Matthias Splitlog

incorporated within the boundaries of Kansas City. His land, a portion of which is still known as Splitlog Hill, is bounded by Barnett and Tauromee Avenues and 4th and 5th streets.

In 1855, the Wyandotte's dissolved their treaty and tribal rights and became citizens of the United States. Unfortunately, many sold during the land rush to Kansas City speculators for far less than its actual value resulting in their potential impoverishment. But fortunately they had an option. Many years before, the Wyandottes had befriended the Seneca Tribe and given them 40 thousand acres of land in Ohio. Since then the Seneca's had relocated to a portion of Indian Territory located in today's Ottawa County, Oklahoma. As a consideration for their former friends, the Seneca's deeded 30,000 acres on their reservation to the Wyandotte Tribe. Most of the tribe moved but the Splitlogs retained their property and continued to live in Kansas City.

Refusing to sell his land to speculators and continuing his inventive genius, Matthias built a steamboat that plied the Missouri River carrying supplies to communities. He also built a saw mill on the Kaw River which proved to be the most fortunate of his ventures. Following the Civil War, when the Union Pacific railroad reached the river, Splitlog received a fabulous sum for the railroad's right of way and other acreage for their railroad shops. After selling another portion of his land in Kansas City to speculators, in 1874 this newly minted "Indian Millionaire" also moved to the new Wyandotte allotment in Ottawa County.

Choosing a site with a spring on the Elk River, Splitlog began construction of the most complete one-man project ever attempted in Northeastern Oklahoma which he named Cayuga Springs. Hiring fellow tribesman, his first endeavor was a large blacksmith shop that could provide essential building materials for other projects. This was followed by a three story building housing a buggy and wagon factory. Soon a general store and subscription school were erected along with other dwellings. Having observed the impact that railroads were having on Kansas City and their recent construction in Indian Territory, Splitlog was convinced that in order to become a viable commercial center Cayuga Springs needed to be connected to a railroad. Consequently, in 1887 a three million dollar building project, "the Splitlog line" was initiated from Joplin, Missouri to Neosho then was proposed to be built on to "Splitlog City," a town he founded in Northeastern Arkansas. Unfortunately the dream began to unravel when a previous investment, the Splitlog Land and Mining Company designed to further fund the railroad and the new community was discovered to have been developed under false claims. The trusting millionaire had been bilked out of his fortune by others who "salted" the so-called mines with gold dust.

Although his fortune was considerably reduced, Matthias Splitlog continued to maintain influence, when in 1890 he was adopted into the Seneca Tribe, elected Chief and made several trips to Washington on their behalf. But in fact, his most enduring legacy was yet to come.

In 1892, Father William Ketcham arrived in Indian Territory and Matthias' wife Eliza, a devout Quaker was converted to Catholicism. Unfortunately, she also was ill with cancer and died the following year. Perhaps it was the combination of these circumstances that inspired him, but in 1893 he began construction of what would become the Cayuga Mission Church. It was dedicated in 1896 to St. Matthias the apostle who replaced Judas after the betrayal of Jesus Christ. It remained as a worship center in the Catholic Diocese until 1930 when it was sold to the Methodist Church. It remains functioning today, historically symbolic of one man's efforts and accomplishments on behalf of his people.

The contributions of Matthias Splitlog toward the betterment of his people are a unique chapter in the history of Northeastern Oklahoma. The fact that his innate intelligence and creative genius enabled him to accumulate millions of dollars is only surpassed by his incredible acts of generosity. For over two decades he financed and promoted projects that would sustain and be beneficial to his fellow tribesmen. Nieberding[8] describes the enthusiasm of Matthias Splitlog as, "Still looking for the promised land-the land of final settlement when he came to Indian Territory." As events developed, he did what he could with the considerable resources he had at his disposal.

Isaac Charles Parker

Judge Isaac Parker, may well be universally the most familiar figure among the Pathfinders of the 19th century in Oklahoma. Books and movies have elevated the "Hangin' Judge," his court and the exploits of his deputies to national, perhaps even international visibility. Born in 1838 near Barnesville, Ohio, a small community 23 miles west of Wheeling, West Virginia, Isaac was the youngest son of farmers Joseph and Jane Parker. As a young man he taught primary school then turned to the legal profession and passed the bar exam in 1859. His uncle D.E. Shannon operated a law firm in St. Joseph, Missouri, and moving west young Parker joined the firm. He met and married Mary O'Toole in St. Joseph and the couple had two sons, Charles and James.

Establishing himself as a successful lawyer in the firm then entering the political arena, in 1861 Parker was elected city attorney for St. Joseph and served several terms until becoming judge of the 12th Missouri Circuit Court. In 1870 he was elected as Republican candidate for Congress and served two terms until 1874. As a Republican congressman he became well known to President Ulysses Grant and in 1875 was appointed judge of the federal court for the Western District of Arkansas located in Fort Smith.

Judge Parker's predecessor at Fort Smith, William Story, as well as several of his deputies, proved to have been both incompetent and corrupt. Few arrests were made and even fewer cases were tried. In 1874, after 14 months, Story resigned for allegedly

Isaac Charles Parker

receiving bribes. Jurisdiction issues in the Western District Court were confusing. Although the legal systems of the Native American tribes in Indian Territory covered their own citizens, federal laws applied to non-Indians. The territory that was involved was huge. The Federal Western District in Arkansas bordered Indian Territory that covered 74,000 square miles, an area that essentially describes Oklahoma. Thus, Isaac Parker was challenged with correcting an ineffective judicial system that covered an enormous area populated by thousands of citizens, some of whom would prove to be the dregs of humanity.

Railroads had recently been completed across Northeastern Oklahoma from north to south and as far west as Vinita, offering easy access for anyone to move regardless of their motive. Of course, most were law abiding citizens but conversely some were brutal criminals who quickly took advantage of the conflicting laws. In an effort to begin to stem the tide of felons, Parker responded quickly and during his first term he tried 18 and convicted 15. In an unprecedented decision within a few months after his arrival, he also ordered the hanging of six at one time. Needless to say, that action attracted not only regional, but national attention. The "Hangin' Judge" as Parker became known had arrived. During his twenty one years on the bench at Fort Smith, a total of 79 men would ultimately hang, twenty two from Northeastern Oklahoma. Shirley[3] summarizes his impact:

> In Judge Parker's twenty-one years on the bench, 13,490 cases had been docketed, exclusive of more than 4,000 petty crimes that got no farther than the commissioners' courts. Of this total, 9,454 had been convicted by a trial jury or had entered pleas of guilty and 344 had been tried for offenses punishable by death. Of those 165 had been convicted and 160 sentenced to the gallows.

During his tenure, a total of two hundred deputy marshals, first coordinated by U.S. Marshal Daniel P. Upham, were charged with maintaining law and order among the mixture of Indian and white citizens. However only 45 or 50 were on duty at the same time and a total of 65 were killed in the line of duty. Ordered to bring criminals to justice "alive or dead," the deputies were frequently thwarted by law abiding citizens who either disliked lawmen themselves or were afraid because of reprisals by the criminals. There also was the risk of prisoners escaping during what could be a journey of as much as 300 miles back to Fort Smith. Deputy Marshals were usually accompanied by an assistant who cooked and drove a specially outfitted wagon in which a number of captured felons were chained. The money the deputies earned certainly did not justify the risk to their lives. Standard pay was six cents a mile for expenses...if a receipt could be provided. If a felon died after being apprehended and there were no known relatives, the marshal was expected to bury him at his own expense. If, and only when he delivered a prisoner to Fort Smith, regardless of their crime, the marshal would receive two dollars each. They also had an expense account. All invoices had to be processed in Washington and were frequently delayed. In most instances, a marshal would be fortunate to make $500 a year.

Most important, through Parker's influence and action, respect for the law in Indian Territory gradually returned and a basic tenant of civilization, the rule of law was re-established. And the leadership of Native American tribes grew to know and appreciated his contribution within their respective areas of jurisdiction. When Parker died on November 17, 1896, at the age of 58, many accolades were offered during his funeral but none so poignant as that of one Indian Chief in attendance. Shirley notes, "But the most touching tribute was paid by Pleasant Porter, Principal Chief of the Creeks who, in behalf of the tribes of all of the Nations, placed upon his grave a simple garland of wild flowers."

On occasion, history reflects that the right person appears at the right time to resolve what has seemingly become an unmanageable task. Isaac Parker fulfills that description. After arriving on one of the most chaotic situations imaginable, within months Parker established himself as a stern but conscientious defender of the law. As years passed his reputation for fairness, coupled with the relentless pursuit of outlaws through courageous deputies, slowly recaptured the region from a desperate existence.

In addition to applying the law of the land, Isaac Parker was personally self effacing, a humanitarian heavily involved in his community. Throughout his tenure, he was often criticized from afar and one notable interview illustrates how many who came to know him were converted. Shortly before Parker's death, Shirley also reflects on one such incident involving Ada Patterson, a reporter for the St. Louis Republic quoting a member of the Fort Smith bar:

> Judge Parker is learned in the law; he is conscientious of the administration of it. He has a kind heart and a big soul. He is absolutely faithful to his home ties. All I could say of him for days would be summed up in this: He is a good man.

Patterson was convinced, praising his accomplishments in a subsequent article sent to the Republic and repeating the phrase "He is a good man."

Bass Reeves

When Isaac Parker was appointed judge of the Western District of Arkansas he recognized the necessity of hiring capable men to uphold the law and sought the best that were available. They were chosen for their intelligence, knowledge of the territory, use of weaponry and survival skills. Among the 200 deputies that served during his 20 year tenure, usually 40 or 50 during any time period, there was a mixture of white, black and Indian peace officers. Burton[9] lists 22 that were African-American including

Bass Reeves, a former slave who became a legendary figure even among the elite who served during Parker's tenure.

Born in Crawford County, Arkansas north of Van Buren in 1838, Reeves and his family were slaves owned by William Steele Reeves. In 1846 the Reeves family moved across the border of Indian Territory to farm land near Sherman, Texas, where Bass grew to manhood. When the Civil War began, Reeve's son, George, was appointed as a Colonel in the 11th Texas Cavalry and Bass accompanied him as his body servant. After accompanying his master during the early stages of the war, while in Texas a disagreement occurred, the two fought and Bass fled into Indian Territory. Living with the Creek and Seminole tribesmen he acquired a wife Jennie and four children. When the war was concluded and he was a freedman, he moved back to Crawford County, Arkansas, and became a farm laborer. Reeves also began assisting federal law enforcement officers as a scout and tracker and from this income he purchased a small farm near Van Buren. Reeve's abilities as a woodsman coupled with the knowledge that he was a skilled marksman apparently convinced U.S. Marshal Daniel P. Upham to appoint him as a deputy marshal in 1875.

Accompanied by a posse man driving a wagon specifically designed with chains to hold prisoners, the deputies were well aware of the no man's land that faced them after leaving Fort Smith. According to some, the boundary line of safety ended when they crossed the north-south Katy railroad tracks at Muskogee on their way west. From that point until reaching Fort Lawton, it was open season on deputy marshals.

Reeves' career from the time of his appointment is a mixture of routine and spectacular arrests. Frequently he pursued criminals accused of selling whiskey illegally, in fact most of the cases brought before Parker involved whiskey. But there were also larceny, bribery or horse theft cases and arrests or occasional shoot-outs involving murder. Disguising himself as a tramp, Bass once walked 28 miles to the mother's home of two known killers. Taking him in for the night and after her two boys were asleep

Reeves managed to handcuff them both and, with the mother walking after him for a few miles yelling obscenities, returned the two 28 miles back to his camp and then brought both to Fort Smith.

In 1884 Bass was involved in seven deadly shoot-outs and there was one in particular he never forgot. During a gunfight, in his attempt to capture murderer Jim Webb, Webb's first shot grazed his saddle horn, the second cut a button from Reeve's coat, and a third cut both of the bridle reins he was holding and a fourth went through the brim of his hat. Bass fired twice and Webb fell mortally wounded. But it was also a year of "business as usual." On July 4th of that same year the *Arkansas Gazette* made note that Reeves and another deputy marshal had returned to Fort Smith with twelve prisoners, five charged with intent to kill, five with larceny and two for peddling whiskey. Later, reporting on September 2 the paper noted Reeves arrived alone in Fort Smith with 15 more.

Reeve's most notable efforts at law enforcement in Northeastern Oklahoma involved Ned Christie and Bob Dozier. With the assistance of his family and friends Christie, who was charged with the murder of Deputy Marshal Dan Maples, had eluded lawmen for three years. But when federal authorities granted a $1,000 reward Reeves decided to attempt to apprehend him. Accompanied by additional posse members, he attacked Christie at his home and succeeded in burning it down. Assuming the outlaw had been consumed in the fire, Reeves returned to Fort Smith only to find Christie had miraculously escaped. One of the few times Bass "didn't get his man."

Bob Dozier was a criminal by choice. A successful farmer, he turned to a diversified life of crime that included stealing cattle, robbing banks and holding up stage coaches. His became a large scale business in which bribes paid a large part and helped him avoid capture. Reeves followed Dozier for several months and finally traced him to his camp in the Cherokee Hills. Ambushed by the Dozier gang, Reeves and his followers hid among the

Bass Reeves

trees. When gunshots rang out, Reeves pretended to be hit and fell to the ground. When Dozier approached him Bass rolled over and fired killing Dozier instantly.

In 1893 Bass Reeves was transferred to Paris, Texas, and continued his manhunt for dangerous criminals, still making regular trips to Fort Smith with his captives. Records are unclear but apparently he was separated from his wife Jennie who died a few years later. Reeves, stationed at various sites in the Indian Nation nearly always succeeded in "getting his man." During this period of time several federal courts were established in the Indian Nation and Bass was assigned to one at Muskogee in 1895. The focus on Judge Parker and the Fort Smith court was coming to a close.

Reeves remarried in 1900 and lived in Muskogee continuing his work as a deputy marshal both in the community and the surrounding area. Muskogee was notorious for criminal activity. Burton notes that "The majority of killings of deputies in the Indian Territory happened within a fifty mile radius of Muskogee, the wildest town in the west." Reeves not only survived he continued to make arrests, possibly the most notable being that of his son Ben who murdered his wife. Reeves arrested him and Ben was sentenced to life imprisonment but was paroled after serving 12 years, then returned to Muskogee and never remarried.

Reeves died January 11, 1910. Again, according to Burton quoting the *Muskogee Phoenix* that printed his obituary:

> Bass Reeves, colored, for 32 years a deputy United States Marshal in Indian Territory who served under the famous Judge Parker at Fort Smith and later at Muskogee, a man credited with fourteen notches on this gun and a terror to outlaws and desperadoes in the old days, died at home at 816 North Howard street late yesterday at the age of 72. Death was caused by Bright's disease and complications.

Deputy Sheriff Bass Reeves was inducted into the Hall of

Great Westerners at the National Cowboy and Western He
Museum in 1992. He was inducted into the Oklahoma Law
Enforcement Hall of Fame in 2010.

Eli Hickman Bruner

There are few men that focused on law enforcement in
Northeastern Oklahoma more than Deputy United States
Marshal Eli Bruner, better known as "Heck." A resident of
Vinita, Indian Territory, for nine and one half years before his
untimely death by drowning, Bruner consistently 'got his man.'
He enjoys the rare distinction of being a lawman to have a
cemetery named after him.

Born February 13, 1859, in Mercer County, Missouri, he was
one of the ten children of Eli and Polly Bruner. When Heck
was 11 the family moved to Siloam Springs, Arkansas where he
grew to manhood. He met and married Sarah Bradley in 1881
and, for the next several years the couple also made their home
in Siloam Springs and raised three children.

Appointed as Deputy United States Marshal in 1890, Bruner
moved to Vinita to allow easier access to the general area he
policed under the jurisdiction of Judge Isaac Parker. Heck soon
learned that the role of marshal was more often apprehending
petty criminals for their mundane offenses than capturing those
involved in capital crimes. His official record is permeated with
everyday arrests and convictions involving illegal sale of liquor,
arson, larceny, bigamy, incest, and assault. These crimes still
required frequent 90 mile trips to Fort Smith accompanying the
offenders and creating long absences from his home in Vinita.
Infrequently and for various reasons he trailed criminals much
further. In 1892 Bruner assisted other lawmen in apprehending
two killers on the Barren Fork River 20 miles east of Tahlequah
nearly 70 miles from Vinita. In 1894 he traveled to Marietta
south of present day Ardmore, Oklahoma and arrested C. E.

Eli Hickman Bruner

Taylor on charges of larceny.

Bruner joined one of the largest group of deputy marshals to be assembled in November of 1892 when a successful attempt was finally made to bring Cherokee outlaw Ned Christie to justice. Christie was accused of shooting Deputy U.S. Marshal Dan Maples five years earlier and had eluded numerous posses since that time. Gathering a safe distance from Christie's cabin in November of 1892, the posse moved in and engaged in a gun battle that included the use of a small cannon, but that proved to be of no avail. Finally, aided with a dozen sticks of dynamite that set the cabin on fire, the marshals killed Christie as he tried to escape the burning inferno.

Judge Parker's deputy marshals went wherever the trail of the criminal took them and did whatever was necessary to apprehend them, but on at least one occasion Bruner just happened to already be at the right place at the right time. Traveling to Fort Smith during October of 1894, he boarded the train at Vinita intent on getting some rest during the journey. Ernst[10] describes what happened later involving the infamous Bill Cook Gang.

> At Wagoner, the train was switched onto the Valley railroad line and continued toward Fort Smith. As it came to the Coretta switch, located between Wagoner and Fort Gibson, the train ran onto the siding and crashed into several boxcars that were parked there. The crash was severe enough to throw most of the passengers onto the floor or under the seats in front of them...four bandits entered the passenger car, but had confronted only a few when an alarm came that a freight train was approaching...Heck Bruner grabbed his rifle and jumped off the sleeper. He found he was on the side where the outlaw's horses were located. As the bandits ran from the train to their horses, Bruner opened fire...

Ernst goes on to explain that after the bandits rode off, the engineer backed the train several miles to Wagoner leaving

Bruner and several others to walk back. He didn't catch the bandits but he foiled the robbery.

Bruner didn't necessarily need to leave the Vinita area to find trouble. While tracking a band of cattle rustlers and bank robbers he discovered they were operating out of White Oak, a small town ten miles southwest of Vinita. Bruner and his posse hid themselves and when two of the gang rode up, gunplay resulted in one being killed, while the other was captured and taken to Fort Smith. In another incident, a Katy (Missouri, Kansas & Texas) railroad train was robbed at Seminole and area bad man Bob Rogers and his gang were suspected of committing the crime. Bruner and his posse found the gang at Rogers' father's farm home near Vinita. A gun fight ensued, one man was killed and Rogers and the rest were arrested, taken to Fort Smith and jailed.

Major events and minor incidents continued to shape the pattern of Bruner's life. And, as arrests continued and gunplay occurred, criminals who challenged him frequently died. Bruner continued to enforce the law and contribute to his legacy until the summer of 1899. Carrying several warrants that he intended to serve for the Muskogee Federal Court, on June 22 he reached the west bank of the Grand River only to discover that West's ferry boat was tethered on the other bank and he could see it was unattended. Impatient, he undressed deciding to swim to the ferry boat and return it so he could board his horse and cross over. Unfortunately he drowned in the rain swollen river and his body was recovered further downstream near the mouth of Little Spavinaw Creek the next day.

Heck Bruner was buried at Graham Memorial Cemetery in Pryor following a procession numbering over 200 local citizens. Stores in the community remained closed in his honor. Recently in 2013, Bruner was inducted into the 4th class of the Oklahoma Law Enforcement Hall of Fame located in Oklahoma City.

Ezekiel Downing Proctor

Ezekiel Proctor represents a different but not uncommon kind of 19th century Pathfinder who might be an enigma by societal standards of today, but not so unusual in the Northeastern Oklahoma of yesterday when some found themselves on both sides of the law. Born July 4, 1831, in Georgia, the son of William and Dicey Proctor, at the age of eight Ezekiel or "Zeke" and his family were crowded onto flatboats for the journey to Indian Territory. Landing at Webber's Falls the family relocated to present day Adair County. He grew to manhood on the family farm northwest of Watts along the eastern border of the Cherokee Nation and gained a reputation for being tough and unpredictable but fair. During a community dance Zeke got into a shooting altercation with the Jay brothers, killing one and wounding the other. And, after one binge while on his way home, he forced his way into a house where a young girl was playing the piano and made her continue, threatening her at gunpoint. Frequently involved in bar fights, Zeke would return the next morning and pay for any damages he caused.

After the Civil War began and when John Ross fled to Kansas in 1862, Zeke an active member of the Keetoowah Society that supported Ross, joined the Union forces in Kansas. He was assigned to Captain Scraper's company of the First Indian Regiment serving as a spy, scout and sharpshooter. Mustered out of the army May 31, 1865, according to his military record, Proctor participated in 35 conflicts including Honey Creek and both of the battles at Cabin Creek.

Zeke was known to have fathered children by three other women but after returning to the family farm following the war, he married Rebecca Mitchell and the couple had five children including triplets. During this time he served one term as district sheriff and from all appearances he had settled down, but in fact the most defining moment in Zeke Proctor's life was about to occur.

Ezekiel Proctor

There are several versions regarding the details of the incident but apparently Jim Kesterson, Zeke's brother-in-law, left his family to court Polly Beck, a widow and owner of the Hilderbrand Mill. On February 13, 1872, after confronting Kesterson at the mill, gunplay ensued and Zeke wounded him but accidentally shot and killed Polly when she stepped between the two men. Recognizing the seriousness of the situation, Zeke immediately reported the accident to the local sheriff, however it became volatile, both because of Polly's relatives who were intent on revenge and the fact that Zeke, a Cherokee Indian had shot Kesterson who was white. In a perfect example of legal confusion at that time, according to federal law the case should be tried in Fort Smith, whereas Indian authorities determined Zeke would be tried for Polly's death in the Goingsnake Indian Territory District.

For security reasons the trial, scheduled for April 15th was moved from the Goingsnake District Courthouse to the Whitmire School further east. In the meantime, the Beck family secured a federal warrant for Proctor to be tried at Fort Smith and a posse that included two United States marshals and several Beck family members were sent to observe the outcome of the trial. Before the trial even started a gun battle ensued and 11, mostly posse members, including several Becks were killed. The event became known as the "Goingsnake Massacre". The trial was resumed the next day and Proctor was found not guilty. Immediately Zeke and his supporters went into hiding and numerous attempts were made to capture him. According to some sources an estimated 25 deputy marshals were killed in the effort.

Since both the United States and the Cherokee Nation argued over jurisdiction of the case, the debate eventually involved Congress and then President Ulysses Grant. Following several failed legal efforts to resolve the situation, over a year after the massacre, Zeke Proctor and his supporters were granted total amnesty by the United States government, the only such action ever granted.

Whether Proctor's popularity within the Nation stemmed from the issues that surrounded him or for other reasons his life following the Goingsnake Massacre changed dramatically. In 1877 he was elected as a senator for the Cherokee Nation representing the Flint District. Later, in an unusual turn of events he served as a deputy marshal for Judge Isaac Parker from 1891 to 1894 and sheriff of the Flint District in 1894. Continuing to farm along the eastern border of the Cherokee Nation for the next several years, Zeke Proctor, farmer, erratic drunk, soldier, gunman, legislator and lawman died of pneumonia February 23, 1907 in bed.

The life adventures of Zeke Proctor although dramatically different than most life styles of today, was not atypical during the 19th century. Disagreements and the gunplay that often occurred characterized the lives of many settlers. And issues that resulted in gunplay were often brought on by too much alcohol not malice of forethought. In fact, if the incident at Hilderbrand Mill had not occurred, Proctor may never have gained the loyalty of his fellow citizens or the attention of historians.

Zeke Proctor is representative of a significant number of settlers in Northeastern Oklahoma who survived the early years essentially on their own terms. The sequence of his life activities reflect both the difficulties and potential of a developing Cherokee Nation. In the beginning, because of the limited scope of government, it often became necessary for each settler to defend his family and himself and maintain a civilized relationship with others while using his own interpretation of the law. Then years after the Civil War as peaceful resolutions to differences were adopted, citizens could become more dependent on "the rule of law" and men, exemplified by Zeke Proctor could, and did, conform to them.

Ned Christie (Ne-de Wa-de)

It may seem unusual to include Pathfinder Ned Christie, more commonly known as a criminal and desperado, among the selected biographies of 19th century Nation Builders. As his story unfolds it will remain the reader's prerogative to render judgment on his inclusion.

Christie was Born December 12, 1852, in Wauhillau Village along Bidding Springs Creek in present day Adair County and grew up in a traditional Cherokee home. His parents were Watt Christie and Watt's third wife Lydia. Watt, an accomplished blacksmith and gunsmith, relocated from North Carolina in 1838. He was very bitter over the loss of the family home in North Carolina and events related to the Trail of Tears. Watt's opinion of circumstances leading to removal during his formative years undoubtedly influenced his son. During Ned's youth he was also surrounded by others that shared his father's beliefs. There was constant discussion about tribal government issues so Ned was imbued with their opinions on Cherokee rights and traditions as well as incidents of federal interference. When Ned was only seven, in 1859 Baptist Missionary Evan Jones and several Cherokee traditionalists, led the effort to reorganize a Cherokee political and spiritual body known as the Keetoowah Society which Watt Christie and his friends quickly joined. The Society promoted traditional Cherokee values and soon acquired a large following. Since the meetings were held nearby, young Ned attended and became further inculcated with Cherokee rights and traditions.

When Ned was nine, Watt left the family home to fight in the Civil War, first he signed on as a Confederate, but following other Keetoowah members soon aligning with the Union. Ned, like most youngsters of that era, remained at home maintaining the farm and protecting his loved ones as best he could. Upon returning safely after the war, Watt gave Ned two matching pistols, ironically he was holding them both when he was killed

Ned Christie

27 years later.

Growing to manhood around Wauhillau and now 6' 4", Ned became an expert woodsman and marksman. He also was an articulate spokesman for traditional values and began to engage in Cherokee politics. Eventually that led to his election at the age of 33 as a representative of the Goingsnake District to the National Council, a body comparable to the United States Senate. His impassioned speeches usually focused on Cherokee rights and responsibilities as well as warnings of continued federal infringement, making him a popular figure among conservatives. During his tenure in office Ned and his constituents agreed as the United States government authorized construction of railroads in the early 1870s despite the protests from the Cherokee leadership. As fellow members of the Keetoowah he and Watt became involved in Zeke Proctor's trial in 1872 and he became further convinced of the injustice represented by the federal government. Ned was aware of the conflicts between Cherokee law and those that seemed to protect white settlers from receiving appropriate punishment when they committed criminal acts in the Nation. And, like others he was very frustrated over the number of white squatters that were moving into the Cherokee Nation also seemingly sheltered by federal laws. When he was elected to the National Council in 1885, statehood for Indian Territory had become a highly debated topic in the United States senate. That was the same year that white squatters west of the Cherokee Nation fenced off large segments of Indian land isolating strategic watering holes while Congress did little to stop it. Situations such as these spurred Ned to make impassioned speeches about ways to prevent further white violations in Indian Territory.

But at some point during his tenure on the Council Ned Christie's attitude and enthusiasm changed. Perhaps he began to recognize the futility to insulate the Cherokee Nation from the federal government when news came of an event in 1886 that was unrelated to local problems, the arrest and imprisonment of

Chief Geronimo, a long time holdout for the Apache Nation. Was the government intent on destroying all tribal leaders? Or, more likely the news of February, 1887 that Congress continued to meddle in the affairs of Indian Nations by approving the General Allotment or Dawes Severalty Act that was destined to divide the land and disregarding the ancient law of mutual property ownership. Regardless, just three months later, undoubtedly discouraged and disenchanted with government interference, Ned Christie would become involved in a life changing event that still remains the subject of debate.

On May 4, 1887, Dan Maples, a popular deputy U.S. marshal from Bentonville, Arkansas, and his posse were encamped along the creek near Tahlequah. Maples, accompanied by George Jefferson, went into town to inquire about a suspected killer. Maples also learned that Jennie Schell had been illegally selling liquor at her home nearby. Returning either to camp or headed for Schell's house at dusk, Maples was shot several times, taken to a Tahlequah residence and died the next morning.

Ned Christie had been drinking at Schell's and, according to reports, he and a friend, John Parris left before the shooting, both very drunk. Accounts vary regarding the accusations that followed, but law enforcement officials became convinced that Christie killed Maples. After declaring his innocence over a period of several weeks, Ned abandoned efforts to convince authorities and became a fugitive. Thus began a one man war lasting nearly five years involving Christie who was pitted against a bevy of United States deputy marshals. His situation also became a call to action for other Cherokee traditionalists, who viewed the charges against him as typical of the many injustices that occurred since removal. And they assisted in protecting him by establishing a network of warning signals triggered at the approach of any lawmen. Coupled with the aid of his friends, his skills as a woodsman and the multiple attempts of lawmen to arrest him, Ned's reputation became larger than life, the ultimate Cherokee warrior of years past. He was a symbol, a living folk hero, said to be able to disappear from confrontations by disguising himself as an animal or bird. As time passed, the crimes of others were also attributed to him and seemingly he was everywhere, but nowhere. Fellow Cherokee found solace from their frustrations with the federal government when learning of his exploits in evading lawmen, real or rumored. From the close of the Civil War a sequence of events occurred that seemed to indicate they were losing their Nation, and now the Cherokee found comfort through the exploits of a defiant and seemingly indestructible hero.

Other events occurred substantiating concerns of members of the Cherokee Nation during Ned Christie's defiant stance. During the summer of 1889 the first land run in the unassigned lands of Indian Territory drew 50,000 white settlers. In 1890 Oklahoma Territory was established by Congress and in 1891 and the spring of 1892 nearly four million more acres of land were opened. Federal courts were initiated in Indian Territory and towns predominantly inhabited by white settlers literally sprung up overnight. Nothing it seemed could stop the intrusion on sovereignty or the surge of newcomers.

So the eyes of many Cherokee traditionalists were focused on Christie, their ultimate warrior who consistently defied death at the hands of his pursuers. He was the one bright spot in an otherwise consistent list of dismal news events seemingly affecting the future of their Nation. He was indestructible, a free, self-sufficient warrior who could win battles regardless of the odds and, as such, he represented their escape from reality.

Then it was over. After what seemed to have been countless encounters including three major attempts by large bands of marshals, on November 3, 1892, Ned Christie was finally trapped and killed while facing insurmountable odds. His body was recovered and displayed on the cellar door of his house. After he was taken to Fort Smith for verification of his death and authorities exulted, three days later he was buried in Christie Cemetery near Wauhillau. The ultimate warrior was dead, but a legend was born that gave Cherokee citizens both an escape and pride during those desperate times at the close of the 19th century. Fifteen years later the dream that had become their sovereign Nation would be absorbed into the new state of Oklahoma.

But the legend surrounding Ned Christie and perhaps justifying his resistance like his ghost-like movements through the forests around Biting Springs Creek, reappeared 35 years later. In 1922, Dick Humphrey, an African American who worked as a blacksmith in Tahlequah confessed to an Oklahoma City reporter that he witnessed the murder of Dan Maples. While headed to Jennie Schell's for a drink of whiskey himself, Humphrey saw Bud Trainor, a friend of Schell's murder Maples.

Humphrey believed it was because Trainor thought the deputy was on his way to arrest Schell. Humphrey, fearing for his own life had remained silent for all those years.

Whether Ned Christie was guilty of Dan Maple's murder or the belated confession by Dick Humphrey exonerated him can be debated but Christie will continue to remain a Cherokee folk hero to many. His long battle against an unwanted authority that continually infringed on the sovereignty of the Cherokee Nation, symbolized the collective frustrations of those that, despite their own good faith effort to build a nation, believed they had once again been cheated by the United States government.

Arthur Edward Stilwell

Northeastern Oklahoma boasts a lengthy list of individuals leaving their footprint who either became residents or simply passed through and Arthur Edward Stilwell was one of the latter. Born in Rochester, New York on October 21, 1859, Stilwell grew up in a privileged family. His grandfather was one of the founders of the New York Central Railroad and was involved in the construction of the Erie Canal.

His father was a medical doctor who later became a jeweler and both parents were active socially. As a youth Arthur suffered from poor health and only attended public school through the 4th grade, privately tutored after that.

In 1879 he courted and married Jennie Wood. The couple moved to Kansas City, then Chicago where he sold insurance for the Travelers Insurance Company. Showing a flare for innovation, he developed a coupon annuity life insurance policy that paid the holder after a certain age. The bonus for creating the policy allowed the couple to move back to Kansas City where he founded a real estate company. Stilwell also took advantage of the housing boom there by constructing low cost homes. Again demonstrating he could "think outside the box," the mortgage for the home came with the provision that it would be cancelled upon the death of the home owner.

Through various community activities, Stilwell became acquainted with Edward Martin, former mayor of Kansas City and owner of a wholesale liquor business. Martin also held the franchise for a forty mile railroad beltway around Kansas City and enlisted Arthur to help raise capital to build it. It was during this effort that the two conceived of the idea of building a railroad from Kansas City to the Gulf of Mexico. Initiated in 1887, the long term venture was soon underway but by the summer of 1893 the country was in the midst of an economic depression. Consequently, the project took on greater significance because the hard times dictated a need for a cheaper way to get regional agricultural products and other resources such as lumber and coal to new markets.

Relying once more on his creativity, Stilwell persuaded investors from Philadelphia as well as others from Holland and England to join in the venture. While Martin concentrated on buying or leasing existing railroad properties, Stilwell developed or purchased several construction companies to lay track between those that existed. His surveyors also platted communities along the route and the pair reaped enormous profits speculating on

Arthur Edward Stilwell

the sales of lots in these new locations. Numerous towns like Gentry, Mena and De Queen, Arkansas and several in Louisiana were named for investors. Stilwell also included himself naming both Stilwell in Adair County and Port Arthur in Texas.

Building a railroad cross country was a tedious undertaking. In fact the venture would span a period of ten years until, according to Vanhooser[11], "At 3:30 P.M. September 11th, 1897 the last spike on the line was driven just 12 miles north of Beaumont, Texas." However the dream that Stilwell and Martin finally saw come true soon turned to a nightmare. Following its completion, lawsuits, a hurricane and yellow fever caused daunting financial problems for the railroad. In 1899 it was thrown into receivership and Stilwell lost out. Later he attempted to manage construction of a railroad to Mexico City, but the Mexican Revolution of 1910-20 caused that company to also go bankrupt.

With this second loss in 1912 Arthur retired to New York City with Jennie but more personal difficult times lie ahead. As the result of an elevator accident, Arthur became an invalid but still maintained his flair for creativity by writing books, plays, poems and hymns mostly for his own satisfaction. When he died in 1928, his fortune was greatly diminished. Despondent over his death, 13 days later Jennie committed suicide by jumping from a window of their apartment. The couple did not have children and there were no near relatives to claim the bodies, so the remains of both Arthur and Jennie were cremated, then eventually misplaced and lost. With neither grave nor memorial Arthur Stilwell's most enduring legacy is the town he named after himself and the railroad running through Northeastern Oklahoma bound for Texas.

Like his predecessor Robert Stevens, General Manager of the Katy railroad, Stilwell was not interested in becoming a resident of Northeastern Oklahoma. Both men were creative entrepreneurs, seizing the moment to acquire wealth then moving on to a new venture. Still, the impact of Stilwell's dream is evident every day along the eastern border of Oklahoma, the memorial to the ingenuity of a man who otherwise might be lost in the annals of history. The Kansas City Southern Railway remains as a contributor to economic development and communities along a corridor from Kansas City to the Gulf of Mexico just as it was envisioned.

BIBLIOGRAPHY

[1]Foreman, Grant. *Early Trails Through Oklahoma*. Chronicles of Oklahoma. Volume 3, No. 2. Oklahoma Historical Society. Oklahoma City, June, 1925. P. 117.

[2]Carter. Kent. *The Dawes Commission and the Allotment of the Five Civilized Tribes, 1893 – 1914*. Ancestry. Com. Orem, Utah. 1999. P. 2.

[3]Shirley, Glen. *Law West of Fort Smith*. Eastern National. Fort Washington, Pennsylvania. 205. P. 198. P. 203. P. 46. P. 206.

[4]*The Tulsa Tribune*. Section Two, Page Thirteen. Saturday, Sept. 19, 1964.

[5]Bell, Watie. *Genealogy of Old and New Cherokee Indian Families*. Original author, George Morrison Bell, Sr. 1972. Republished by The Covington Group, Kansas City, Mo. 2003 and 2006.

[6]Parker, Robert Dale. *American Indian Poetry*. University of Pennsylvania Press. Philadelphia, Pennsylvania. 2011. P. 38.

[7]Masterson V. V. *The Katy Railroad and the Last Frontier*. University of Missouri Press. Columbia and London. 1952. P. 113-114.

[8]Nieberding, Velma. *Chief Splitlog and the Cayuga Mission Church*. Chronicles of Oklahoma. Vol. 32-1. Oklahoma Historical Society. 1954. P. 18-19.

[9]Burton, Art T. *Black Gun, Silver Star The Life and Legend of Frontier Marshal Bass Reeves*. University of Nebraska Press.

Lincoln and London. 2006. P. 4. P. 7. P. 298.

[10]Ernst, Robert. *Heck Bruner, Deputy U.S. Marshal of the Indian Territory*. Journal of the Fort Smith Historical Society, Inc. Vol. 35, No. 2. September, 2011. P.12.20.

[11]Vanhooser, Howard C. *History of Adair County*, First Edition. Historical Societies of Adair County. Arc Press. Cane Hill, AR. 1991. P. 7.

Index

Guthrie 58

H

Hale, Nathaniel 38
Harpe, Benard de la 12, 13
Henley, Elizabeth 79
Hilderbrand Mill 173
Hitchcock, Annie 10
Hitchcock, Ethan Allen 79, 125
Homestead Act 149
Hopefield Mission 96, 108
Horseshoe Bend 48
Houston, Samuel 41, 46, 50, 51,
    52, 65, 67, 68

I

Independence 54
Indian Removal Act 70, 94
Irving, Washington 4, 5, 37, 46,
    50, 58, 59, 60, 108

J

Jackson, Andrew 40, 48, 51, 62,
    63, 72, 74, 76, 94, 118
Jefferson, Thomas 23, 25, 26, 38,
    42
Jefferson Barracks 55
Jenks 12
Johnson County 63
Jolly, John 48, 50, 65, 67, 68, 102
Jones, Evan 110, 111, 113, 114,
    115, 121, 122, 124, 129, 177

K

Kansas 3, 15, 25
Kansas City 27, 33, 54
Kaskaskia 16, 18, 19, 35
Keetoowah Society 113, 129, 177
Kesterson, Jim 173
Ketcham, William 157

Kiersereau, Pelagie 42
Kingsbury, Cyrus 94
Kiowa village 5
Kirby-Smith, E. 87
Knights of the Golden Circle 113

L

Labadiea, Sophie 44
Laclede 21
La Saline 14, 22, 23, 24, 36, 42,
    44, 45, 46, 47
Latrobe, Charles 58
Leadville, Colorado 44
Lewis, Anna 17
Lewis, Meriwether 23, 38
Lewis and Clark expedition 41
Liguest, Pierre Laclede 19
Lisa, Manuel 22, 24
Louisiana 3, 16, 21
Louisiana Purchase 14, 15, 21, 23,
    24, 30, 31, 33, 38, 65, 74,
    102
Louisiana Territory 42
Love, Hugh 36
Lovely's Purchase 64, 106
Lovely, William 64, 106, 109

M

Mankiller, Wilma 11
Maples, Dan 165, 169, 178, 180
Marcy, Ralph 4
Martin, Edward 181, 183
Martin, Joseph 9, 139, 142, 143,
    144, 145
Martin, Richard 143
Mayes County 6
Mexico 3, 27, 33
Mexico City 2, 28
Military Road 56, 134
Mississippi 2, 3, 16, 32

Ross Cemetery 82

S

Salina 1, 14
Sallisaw 14
Sallisaw Creek 6
Santa Fe 3, 12, 14, 16, 18, 44, 45, 46, 54
Santa Fe Trail 54
Scott, Winfield 96, 98, 99, 104, 122, 127
Sequoyah 70, 72, 80, 87, 89, 90, 95, 110, 116
Shawnee Trail 33, 135
Shirley, L. W. 10
Sioux City, Iowa 38
Soto, Hernando De 3, 12
Spain 44
Spaniard, Polly 56
Spanish 3
Spavinaw Creek 50
Splitlog, Matthias 154, 156, 157, 158
St. Louis 1, 21, 23, 24, 25, 32, 38, 42, 44, 45, 46, 47, 54, 55, 58
Stevens, Robert 149, 151, 152, 153, 154, 184
Stilwell, Arthur 181, 183, 184

T

Tahlonteskee 63, 64, 65, 101, 102
Takertawker 83
Taovayas 1
Tawakoni Indians 12, 13
Taylor, Richard 97
Texas 3, 28, 33, 42, 51, 52, 60
Texas Road 33, 50, 60, 110, 134, 135, 142, 143, 145, 152
Thomas, Heck 10
Three Forks 4, 5, 6, 12, 14, 27, 30, 31, 32, 33, 35, 36, 37, 38,

45, 64
Tisne, Charles Claude Du 3, 12, 14, 15, 17, 18, 19
Trail of Tears 85, 90, 95, 111, 114, 126, 132
Treaty of Fort Clark 23
Treaty of New Echota 71, 77, 81, 82, 85, 96, 111, 119, 122, 124, 126, 130, 132, 146
Treaty of Paris 19
Treaty Party 56, 71, 72, 75, 80, 81, 86
Tula Indians 3
Tulsa 26, 58

U

Union Mission 6, 40, 96, 105, 106, 108, 109, 110, 119
United Foreign Missionary Society 40
United States Dragoons 55

V

Vaill, William F. 107
Van Bibber, Olive 54
Vann, James 74
Verdigris River 1, 13, 14, 15, 23, 26, 27, 32, 35, 45
Vernon County, Missouri 21

W

Waco 1
Walker, William 6
Ward, Nancy 9
Washburn, Abigail 102
Washburn, Cephas 65, 101, 102, 104, 105, 119
Watie, Stand 56, 81, 83, 85, 86, 87, 143, 146, 148
Watie, Thomas 81
Webber's Falls 32

Made in the USA
Middletown, DE
11 December 2016